The Waters of Oblivion
The British Invasion of the Rio de la Plata, 1806–1807

THE WATERS OF OBLIVION

THE BRITISH INVASION OF THE RIO DE LA PLATA, 1806-1807

by

Ian Fletcher

History will record, and posterity with difficulty will believe that such an army as ours capitulated with the rabble of a South American town ... Would to God the waters of Oblivion were as near at hand as those of La Plata.

Sir Samuel Whittingham

SPELLMOUNT

British Library Cataloguing in Publication Data:
A catalogue record for this book is available
from the British Library

Copyright © Ian Fletcher 2006

ISBN 1-86227-342-1

This edition first published in the UK in 2006 by
Spellmount Limited
The Mill
Brimscombe Port
Stroud
Gloucestershire GL5 2QG

Tel: 01453 883300
Fax: 01453 883233
E-mail: enquiries@spellmount.com
Website: www.spellmount.com

1 3 5 7 9 8 6 4 2

The right of Ian Fletcher to be identified
as the author of this work has been asserted by him
in accordance with the Copyright, Designs
and Patents Act 1988

Printed in Great Britain by
Oaklands Book Services
Stonehouse, Gloucestershire GL10 3RQ

Contents

List of Illustrations   vii

List of Maps   ix

Acknowledgements   x

Introduction   xi

I   To the Rio de la Plata   1

II   The Capture of Buenos Aires   11

III   La Reconquista   25

IV   The Fall of Montevideo   41

V   Whitelocke   61

VI   The March to Buenos Aires   75

VII   La Defensa   93

VIII   Victory and Defeat   113

IX   Aftermath   123

Appendices   131

Endnotes   149

Bibliography   155

Map Section   159

Index   173

List of Illustrations

1. Francisco de Miranda.
2. Sir Home Riggs Popham.
3. The Marquis de Sobremonte.
4. William Carr Beresford.
5. British troops land at Quilmes in June 1806.
6. Beresford's troops enter the outskirts of Buenos Aires.
7. British landings at Quilmes on 25 June 1806.
8. British troops at Lujan on 9 July 1806.
9. La Reconquista. Spanish troops attack Beresford, 12 August 1806.
10. La Reconquista. Beresford surrenders his sword.
11. Town and citadel of Montevideo.
12. The storming of Montevideo, 3 February 1807.
13. Sir Samuel Auchmuty.
14. Robert Craufurd.
15. John Whitelocke.
16. Denis Pack.
17. Francisco Xavier de Elio.
18. Santiago Liniers.
19. Martin de Alzaga.
20. Juan Martin de Pueyrredon.
21. The death of Captain Renny.
22. Attack on Montevideo, 3 February 1807.
23. British soldiers on guard duty outside Montevideo.
24. British troops in Montevideo after its capture.
25. Montevideo surrenders to Sir Samuel Auchmuty.
26. La Defensa. A column of British troops comes under attack.
27. Soldiers from the *Patricios* regiment attacking Craufurd's men.

28. La Defensa. Whitelocke surrenders to Liniers.
29. Linier's volunteer cavalry.
30. Linier's volunteer infantry.
31. A trooper of the 1st Escuadron de Husares.
32. A Miguelte.
33. An officer of the Cazadores de Correntinos.
34. An officer of the *Patricios*.
35. An officer of the Cazadores de la Reyna (4th Husares).
36. An officer of the 2nd Escuadron de Husares (Husares de Vivas).
37. An officer of the Tercio de Vizcainos.
38. An officer of the Granaderos Provinciales.
39. Santiago Liniers execution on 10 August 1810.
40. Whitelocke and the ghost of Admiral Byng.

List of Maps

Provinces of the Rio de la Plata
Operations on the Rio de la Plata
Combat at Point de Quilmes, June 26, 1806
La Reconquista: Liniers' Attack, August 12, 1806
The Montevideo Campaign, Jan/Feb, 1807
Montevideo, February, 1807
The Fight at San Carlos, November 7, 1807
Whitelocke's March, June/July, 1807
The Fight at the Corrale del Miserere, July 2, 1807
La Defensa: The British Attack, July 5, 1807
La Defensa: The Attack by the British Left
La Defensa: Craufurd's Attack

Acknowledgements

With grateful thanks to:

The National Army Museum Chelsea, the British Library and Canning House Library, the National Library of Ireland, the regimental museum and archives of the Worcester and Sherwood Foresters Regiment.

Introduction

The latter part of the eighteenth century had been a busy time for the British army and the tide of war in recent years had taken its soldiers to the deserts of Egypt, to the gloom of the Netherlands, to India and to the West Indies. It was the autumn of 1805 and the British army was about to begin another journey, this time to the bottom of the world, to the Cape of Good Hope, to wrest from the Dutch a colony which Pitt's government had decided had great military and geographical importance for it was seen as the perfect base from which Britain could protect the sea route to her possessions in India and the Far East. And so, on the last day of August that year, some 6,300 men under the command of Sir David Baird set out from Cork, in the south of Ireland, on the long journey south to the Cape, where they would again fight for king and country.

In Sir David Baird the British force had for its leader a hero, he himself having not long returned to England after an almost continual absence of nearly twenty-four years during which time he had become a popular hero at home following the campaign in Egypt in 1801 and his march across the desert.

Baird had started his army career in 1773 as an ensign at the age of sixteen and by 1780 he was a captain, bound for India with the 73rd Highlanders. On his arrival in India Baird found himself with a force under Sir Hector Munro, trying to relieve the city of Arcot which was being besieged by Hyder Ali. During the operations Baird and his men were badly cut up by a force under Ali and his son, Tippoo Sultan. Baird was severely wounded and left for dead but with two other wounded men he managed to find a French camp where he was taken prisoner and his wounds tended. After a while, however, the French were obliged to hand him over to Hyder Ali whose men treated their prisoners with barbaric cruelty. Baird existed in agony for three years, watching fellow prisoners go mad or die of fever. At last, in March 1784, Baird and the remaining prisoners were released and upon rejoining his regiment he was able to extract the bullet which had been lodged in his thigh for the past three years.

In 1801, Baird was given command of a force ordered to assist Sir Ralph Abercromby in Egypt. He reached Cosseir, on the Red Sea, in June 1801, and decided to march across the desert to reach the Nile. The march was undertaken in the most oppressive conditions, it being the middle of summer. It was unknown country and supplies were few, the commissariat having broken down. Notwithstanding these handicaps, however, Baird, with his adjutant, Sir Samuel Auchmuty, who we shall meet later, got the army safely across the desert to reach the Nile. He then got his force down the river in boats to arrive in Cairo three days after its fall to the British.

Back in England, Baird's expedition had caught the imagination of the public, mainly because of the march across the desert. Pictures and cartoons of him were circulated as were tales of his ordeal as a prisoner of Hyder Ali. He was soon a popular hero but his rewards were scant. In 1802 he again returned to India at the approach of the Mahratta War but found he could not fit in under Sir Arthur Wellesley, the future Duke of Wellington, who had great influence in political circles and so he left for England. By the time he returned home he had been away for almost twenty-four years but even now his stay was short. After being promoted lieutenant-general and being knighted by King George III in 1805 he was given command of the force now bound for the Cape of Good Hope.

The convoy carrying the troops to the Cape consisted of sixty-one transports which were escorted by Sir Home Popham's squadron, which included the 74-gun ship *Diadem*, the *Belliquesque*, the *Diomede*, the frigates *Narcissus* and *Leda*, and the gun-brig *Encounter*. By mid-November the ships reached Bahia where one of the transports and a store ship were wrecked while working into the bay. Unfortunately, the commander of the artillery, Brigadier Yorke, with two other men, was drowned in the accident but after making good the losses the ships continued on their way and by 4 January 1806, were off Table Bay.

Two days later, on 6 January, Baird's force began to land at Saldannah Bay. The first troops ashore were those of the Highland Brigade under Brigadier Ferguson. They were unopposed except for a few companies of burgher militia that were kept at a respectful distance by the guns of four of the ships. Although there was no opposition from the Dutch, however, the landings were made extremely hazardous by a violent surf that lifted the boats out of the water. A breakwater was created, therefore, by the running aground of a small transport ship and with the skill of the navy's 'bluejackets' nearly all of the troops got ashore safely. One of the boats was swamped, however, and all thirty-six men belonging to the 93rd Highlanders were drowned. The rest of the force was landed the next day along with the artillery and supplies and soon the whole force began to trudge inland.

The Dutch general, Janssen, was having great difficulty in collecting his troops, particularly as it was harvest time and for the burghers the busiest time of the year. Apart from the burghers Janssen had one battalion of Waldeck mercenaries, about 400 in all, as well as an assortment of European riflemen, dragoons and some artillery, making in total about 1,200 men. Janssen's motley force finally totalled around 2,000 men with sixteen guns, not much of a force with which to face the trained British regulars now marching on Cape Town.

The opposing forces clashed on 8 January on the heights of the Blauberg, and after a brief fight Janssen's army was scattered with losses of around 200 men killed and wounded. With Janssen having been beaten terms of surrender were drawn up and on 18 January they were accepted and Cape Colony signed over to the British.

In all, Baird's expedition had been a great success but it had all been achieved a little too easily for the restless commodore, Sir Home Popham, who soon began to cast his roving eye over the horizon, in particular towards South America and the treasures of the Spanish colony of the Rio de la Plata. Popham, with his acquisitive eye, was about to commit Great Britain to a struggle between herself and the Spanish colony, a struggle that was to last for thirteen months and involve over ten thousand British troops. The conflict was to bring vastly differing fortunes for the two opposing sides and for one British general in particular the consequences were to be serious and far reaching.

The story of the British invasion of the Rio de la Plata is a story of daring, triumph and glory. But it is also one of lost opportunity, disappointment and ultimate failure. It is also the story of one of the most obscure campaigns ever fought by the British army, which is surprising when one considers the names of those British officers who took part in the campaign and later went on to achieve fame later in their careers, particularly under Wellington during the Peninsular War and at Waterloo.

This is the story of that campaign, a campaign which was eventually to lead to the creation of a new nation, Argentina, and was one that would inspire first a nation and then almost a whole continent to rise up and free itself from Spanish rule. For Britain, however, it was an extremely disappointing campaign, which effectively put an end to her aspirations in South America. It is an obscure and long forgotten campaign. The Waters of Oblivion.

I

To The Rio de la Plata

On the morning of 14 October 1804, a carriage pulled up outside a house in the English countryside and as its door swung open two men stepped from it. One was a South American revolutionary and adventurer, and the other a British naval commodore, and although from different backgrounds they shared the same dream, if, however, for different motives. As the South American's secretary unloaded numerous boxes of maps, books and papers the two men set to work and eventually conceived a plan which was to unwittingly involve Britain in an invasion of one of Spain's most prized and richest South American possessions, namely the colony of the Rio de la Plata.

The South American was Francisco de Miranda, a revolutionary who had spent years travelling Europe in an attempt to gain support for his plan to rid his country, Venezuela, of Spanish rule, his ultimate aim being, of course, to see the whole of Spanish America free of the Spanish yoke.

Born in 1750, Miranda was a somewhat shady and dubious character who, in 1782, had been dismissed from Spanish service following his dealings in illicit trading with North America. He had also been guilty of delivering up to the British government the plans of the fortifications of Havana. Ever since his dismissal he had tried to enlist British support for his venture to free the Spanish colonies and in 1783 submitted plans to the British government only to be thwarted by Fox and North. Three years later he tried again and although sympathetically received by Pitt he was still unsuccessful.

In 1796 war broke out between Britain and Spain and once again Miranda approached Pitt and even Lord Grenville for help. This time an expedition was actually prepared but was later abandoned. In 1801, his desperate attempts to seek support took him to France to see Napoleon,

1

but he could gain nothing there and so returned to England the following year. This time Miranda was given great encouragement by Addington, although the British politician stopped short of actually supplying a ship for him. It seemed as though Miranda would never get help, but in 1804 Pitt returned to power and Miranda thought it time to try again and was soon drawing up fresh plans to submit to British ministers.

The country house in which Miranda now stood, stretching out over maps of South America, belonged to the English naval commodore who had been in the carriage with him. His name was Sir Home Riggs Popham and he had met Miranda many years before and had spent countless hours with him pleading and arguing his case to British ministers. Popham, ostensibly the man who was to spark off the British invasions of the Rio de la Plata, was a total advocate of Miranda's plans and had pledged his utmost support. His motives for doing so, however, were sadly very different.

Born in 1762, Sir Home Popham entered the Royal Navy in 1778 and during the next two years saw action off Cape St. Vincent and in the West Indies. After being promoted to lieutenant in 1783 he surveyed the coast of Kaffraria and four years later joined Lord Cornwallis in India where he drew up plans for a naval dockyard at Calcutta. In 1790 he surveyed the island of Pulo Penang and discovered a new channel to the south there. By now he was proving himself as an officer of some ability and had devised a code of naval signals and later drew up a plan for the establishment and organisation of sea-fencibles. More significant, however, was the fact that he was on good terms with many high-ranking people such as the deputy-governor of India and he knew several members of the council there.

Between 1793 and 1794 Popham was attached to the army in Flanders and served under the Duke of York. Here he was entrusted with the charge of gunboats and pontoons and on 24 July 1794, the Duke forwarded to the Admiralty a strong commendation of his conduct and services as superintendent of the inland navigation. He had already gained favour in high places and during this period it increased as he found himself travelling between the Low Countries and London with despatches. Whilst on these duties Popham had always been seen and consulted by ministers and was not afraid to voice his own opinion. In a way, it could be said that he enjoyed some measure of influence with them.

By the turn of the century, Popham had worked so often with the army that he had gained a thorough knowledge and understanding of that service and would go to great lengths to ensure that conditions for the troops with whom he was working were as pleasant as possible. He had also become quite skilful in the field of embarking and disembarking of troops in enemy-held territory. The care he took to ensure the men's welfare made him a popular man in the navy with officers and men alike but the one area which was usually the main object of his concern was, unfortunately, also his weak spot: prize money.

Throughout his career Popham had been employed in more or less independent stations and this had given him a chance to dabble in certain mercantile transactions which were looked upon by those around him as being of a rather dubious nature, the *Etrusco* incident of 1793 and the inquiry, in, early 1804, into the cost of repairs to his ship, the *Rodney*, being examples and it was not long before Popham saw the chance to add to both his wealth and importance following his meeting with Miranda.

The result of the meeting, in fact, was a memorandum, dated 16 October 1804, which set out details for an expedition to South America. With Pitt in power, and remembering that he had previously seemed sympathetic to them, the two men submitted their plan having already gained the support of Lord Melville. The plan involved the co-operation of the people of New Grenada and Venezuela and help was also expected from Miranda's friends in Trinidad which was to be used as a base for the operations.

For the campaign, Miranda requested from the British government two thousand infantry, two corps of dismounted cavalry and two companies of artillery from the troops stationed in the West Indies. These troops were to be assisted by a British squadron that was to include a frigate and a sloop of war. Miranda believed that, once master of his own country, he could raise 20,000 men with whom he would march through New Grenada to the Isthmus of Panama.

Things looked more optimistic when Sir Arthur Wellesley, no less, at the request of ministers, was asked to draw up similar plans for an expedition up the Orinoco. Once again, however, in spite of all the talking, neither Popham nor Miranda could convince the British government to lend a hand in the struggle for freedom in South America and nothing came of the discussions although later, curiously enough, Popham stated that he was left with the impression that he had been given a free hand to act against Buenos Aires. This could only have been as a result of a loose statement made by either Pitt or Melville during one of their frequent discussions with Popham. After all, such a plan appealed to them especially after the way in which Popham argued his case. He said that aid to Miranda would benefit Britain in two ways.

First, that imports from South America into Spain each year were worth some twenty million pounds and that two thirds of this amount passed into the hands of Britain's enemy, France. He also argued that the lucrative South American markets could be opened up to British trade. This last point, however, Miranda thought strange and began to suspect, probably quite correctly in Popham's case, that the latter intended to aid him only in order to obtain trading concessions. Miranda was forced to point out to Popham that if this was the case then the ports would be opened up to every nation but whilst all other people would be treated with freedom and consideration the British would be treated with suspicion.

However, after all the cases had been argued back and forth there was still nothing forthcoming from the British government in terms of action in support of Miranda. Many ministers, Grenville included, mistrusted him. They had not supported him in 1796 and were still not going to do so now. Miranda, therefore, went away empty handed. As one historian later put it Miranda was in truth:

> a shallow, unscrupulous adventurer, not wholly innocent of knavery, and that Popham's character at bottom perhaps differed not very greatly from that of Miranda.[1]

The years of pleading by both Miranda and Popham had come to nothing and if there ever were any plans for the British government to act in support of them they were certainly abandoned in 1805. However, following the capture of Cape Colony from the Dutch, events were to move quickly and the whole question of British involvement in South America to change drastically following an act of almost Elizabethan buccaneering proportions by the adventurous commodore, Popham.

Popham found himself at the Cape with a strong naval squadron and with no special orders other than to protect the sea route around the Cape to India. Therefore, without any immediate task at hand he thought the time right to rekindle his designs for fame and fortune in South America. Popham recalled that during the conversations he had had with Pitt and Melville he had been left with the impression that they had given him a free hand to act against the Spanish colonies in South America and it did not take him long to convince himself that the true purpose of his mission was not, after all, the capture of the Cape but the more glorious expedition against the Spanish colonies and in particular that of the Rio de la Plata.

His first task, however, was to persuade Sir David Baird to let him take a force of men from the Cape's garrison to attack the colony. Baird was a strong-minded Scot who was not easily swayed but it says much for Popham's powers of persuasion that he finally managed to talk him into letting him have a small force consisting of the 71st Regiment, commanded by Lieutenant-Colonel Denis Pack, a small detachment of artillery and some men from the 20th Light Dragoons, the whole of which was to be placed under the command of Brigadier-General William Carr Beresford, later to rise to fame during the Peninsular War where he served with distinction under Wellington and commanded the Portuguese army.

The 37-year old Beresford was the illegitimate son of the Earl of Tyrone, George de la Poer Beresford. He received his first commission in August 1785, and the following year travelled to Nova Scotia with his regiment, the 6th Foot. Whilst there he met with a shooting accident that left him without the sight of his left eye. By 1791 he was a captain and in the middle of that year found himself attached to the 69th Regiment under the command of Vice-Admiral Hotham with the Mediterranean fleet. At Toulon, the various companies of regular troops acting as marines, the 69th, included, were landed in order to garrison the place and Beresford was mentioned in Lord Mulgrave's despatches. When Lord Hood was driven from the city in December 1793, the troops withdrew to Corsica where Beresford commanded the storming party at the tower of Martello, for which he received his brevet-majority in March, 1794. He returned to England in August the same year to be promoted lieutenant-colonel and in September the following year took command of the 88th Regiment.

After a brief period of service in India in 1800 the 88th formed a part of the force under Baird which left for Egypt where it was to join the army there under Sir Ralph Abercromby. Baird's force arrived too late to be of any actual service but as earlier mentioned the march across the desert captured the imagination of the British public and Beresford shared the popularity of Baird, Auchmuty and George Murray. He remained in Egypt until its evacuation in 1803 when he returned to England with a great military reputation and was given command of a brigade at home. When the expedition against Cape Colony was planned Beresford, a man of great strength, was given command of a brigade. Now, instead of contenting himself as part of the garrison there, Beresford found himself bound for the Rio de la Plata as commander of the small force which Popham had managed to persuade Baird to give him in order to attack the Spanish colony there.

In spite of the impending departure of the 71st Regiment there was still a relatively strong garrison left at the Cape, consisting of the 21st Light Dragoons, the 24th, 38th, 72nd and 93rd Regiments, a Hottentot light infantry corps, about three hundred strong, and two companies of the 2nd and 54th Regiments which had been released from captivity on board the French frigate, *La Voluntaire*. This ship had sailed into Cape Town not knowing that the place had been taken by the British and before the mistake was realised the frigate, containing British prisoners, was itself taken and the British troops on board made a welcome addition to the garrison.

Nevertheless, one feels that Baird was still slightly uneasy about the plan to send a force to attack the Spanish colony in the Rio de la Plata. On the very day that Popham and Beresford set sail he sent a despatch to Colonel Gordon, secretary to the Commander-in-Chief, in which he set down his feelings.

In my private letter to you, by *La Voluntaire* frigate, I took occasion to mention that I had been much pressed by Sir Home Popham to detach a regiment with the squadron under his command, for the purpose of making an attack upon the Spanish settlements at Rio de la Plata, but that many reasons combined at the moment to prevent my acquiescence in the Commodore's wish.

The additional intelligence (since) received here of the weak and defenceless condition of those settlements, the great advantages derivable to Great Britain from the possession of them, particularly as opening a fresh and profitable channel for the exportation of our manufactures, the certainty that Admiral Villeneuve has proceeded to India, and for some months interrupt the present tranquillity of this colony, and the rapidly increasing strength and discipline of the Cape regiments, have together united in determining me to detach a small part of the force under my own command upon this service.

I am aware that I have taken upon myself a high responsibility, but the importance of the object in a national point of view will, I trust, bear me out, and ensure me to the approbation of His Majesty, and of His Royal Highness the Commander-in-Chief.

As I deemed it essential to the success of the undertaking that the command should be entrusted to an officer of rank, and of approved ability, judgement, and zeal, I selected Brigadier-General Beresford, although I shall experience by his absence the want of his valuable services.

Having also considered that, in the event of success, the officer discharging the civil and military duties of His Majesty's Lieutenant Governor and Commandant should possess a high military rank, I have taken upon myself to desire that Brigadier-General Beresford should assume, upon landing in South America with the troops under his command, the rank of Major-General in that country only, as the standing of this officer in the service induces the belief of his having already been appointed to that rank by His Majesty, I am the more induced to hope my making this appointment will meet with the approbation of his Royal Highness the Commander-in-Chief.[2]

And so on 14 April 1806, the small British force sailed from Table Bay to begin a campaign totally without any official sanction from the British government whatsoever and a campaign straight from the annals of the buccaneering pirates of the past.

The voyage itself was a difficult one. Popham's squadron had been at sea only six days when suddenly, on the 20th, a violent storm arose which lasted throughout the night. In fact, so violent was the storm that the next morning the transport ship *Ocean* was nowhere to be seen and was feared lost. This was a serious blow to Popham as the ship was carrying 200 men of the 71st Regiment and his force was now so weakened that he put in at St. Helena on 30 April where he hoped to persuade the governor there to reinforce him with some of the men from the island's garrison. Once again, Popham's powers of persuasion paid dividends and he managed to contrive the governor into 'lending' him 100 artillerymen and just under 300 of the St. Helena infantry.

Whilst also at the island both Popham and Beresford wrote letters to England. Beresford asked for instructions as to how he should deal with the local inhabitants, whilst Popham wrote, in a somewhat guilty tone, a long and elaborate letter explaining his actions to William Marsden, Secretary of the Admiralty:

> In consequence of having borne up for St. Helena…I deem it right to trouble you with this letter for their Lordships' information.
>
> To satisfy their Lordships, in the first instance, that the project has not arisen from any sudden impulse, or the immediate desire of gratifying an adventurous spirit, I take the liberty of transmitting for your perusal the copy of a paper which I wrote by the desire of Lord Melville when he was at the Board of Admiralty, after having previously had a conference with Mr. Pitt and his Lordship on that subject if the records of the Admiralty were to be examined, or the still better evidence, the living testimonies of the merchants of London restored to, you will, I have no doubt, find that Buenos Aires is the best commercial station in South America. It is the grand centre and emporium of the trade of all its provinces, and is the channel through which a great proportion of the wealth of the kingdom of Chile and Peru annually passes.
>
> These advantages have been so strongly urged in a provincial weekly publication which I am in possession of, that the Spanish government was obliged to interfere, and stop its further progress; as it was evidently written to invite foreign protection, and to induce Great Britain to profit of the neglected state in which those valuable colonies were left by the mother country…
>
> In addition and corroboration of all the intelligence I obtained last war, Mr. Wilson, an eminent merchant of the city of London, informed me a few days before I left town, and which communication I made to Mr. Pitt, that Monte Video was very defenceless, and that a thousand men would easily obtain possession of that place and Buenos Aires, which is an open town; and that after the Spanish troops were sent from the country, the natives would easily keep possession of it under an amelioration of their export and import duties and some other heavy and oppressive taxes.
>
> …and an Englishman who had been eleven months a ship-carpenter at Monte Video, and had only just arrived in a Spanish vessel, has, under every kind of cross examination, adhered without variation to this account; that there are not above two hundred and fifty regular troops at Monte Video, and some provincial cavalry and militia; that the walls of the town are in a ruinous state; and that he believes the inhabitants would force a surrender without firing a shot.
>
> The expedition will sail tomorrow evening, and we calculate on four weeks passage, but I trust that this small armament will only be

considered as a floating force to keep up the national characteristic enterprise, and ready to apply to any point of the enemy's possessions which have been neglected, provided there is moral certainty of success, and no risk beyond the common calculation under such circumstances.[3]

On 21 May, after taking on its reinforcements, the squadron resumed its journey to the Rio de la Plata and if Popham needed any reassurance as to the wisdom of the expedition, which is highly unlikely, it came when one of his frigates, the *Narcissus*, detained a schooner bound for Spain. On board was a Scotsman named Russell, who had lived in Buenos Aires for the past fifteen years. After being questioned he claimed that a large sum of money had just arrived in the city from the Upper Country and it was shortly to be sent to Spain. He also claimed that the city itself was unprotected, save for a few regular troops and a few companies of undisciplined *Blandengoes*, a popular rabble, adding that the approaching festival of Corpus Christi would hold the attention of the local people, and provide the British troops with a perfect opportunity to land unhindered. Just how much notice Popham took of this dubious information is speculation, but the report of a large sum of money waiting in Buenos Aires would have sorely tempted such a man as himself.

Eventually the squadron anchored off Cape St. Mary, which marks the northern entrance to the river, on 8 June. Popham himself had gone forward on 27 May with a group of officers and engineers to explore the navigation of the channel and reconnoitre the country, albeit from a distance. The rest of the squadron did not overtake him until 14 June owing to the winds and fog. One piece of good news for the British came with the appearance of the transport ship *Ocean* which had gone missing during the storm of 20 April. The ship had not been lost after all but had, in fact, carried on alone.

The Spanish viceroyalty of the Rio de la Plata consisted in 1806 of the greater part of what is now Argentina, as well as the republics of what are now Uruguay, Bolivia and Paraguay. To the west lay the Andes and to the north Brazil. Buenos Aires was the capital of the province and at the time was the major city in South America with a population of about forty thousand people.[4] The city stretched for two miles along the bank of the Rio de la Plata, the mouth of which was 150 miles away. The width of the river at the capital was 28 miles but navigation was made difficult by shoals and mud banks as well as fog and it was impossible for any ship drawing more than fifteen feet of water to approach within eight miles of the shore.

On the opposite bank of the river was the city of Montevideo. The British force would benefit greatly if they could take this place also but the obvious riches that were to be found in Buenos Aires were too tempting for Popham, and the information gleaned from the Scotsman, Russell, however dubious, only convinced him further that the true point of attack should indeed be Buenos Aires. This was a major deviation in the plan because Beresford had intended to occupy Montevideo. This would give him a secure base from which to operate and would give him good protection against any enemy forces who would find the British difficult to dislodge. Also, if it came to the worst, Montevideo would provide the troops with a safe place from which to re-embark. Beresford was also given to assume, on scant information, that the fortifications of Montevideo were in a pretty bad state and that the place would surrender without putting up too much resistance.

Popham, however, had his way and the point of attack was changed from Montevideo to Buenos Aires. The reason he gave for the change was that the troops' bread stocks were exhausted and there would be a greater chance to re-stock in the latter. This may well have been true but it is safer to assume that Popham knew the financial rewards to be greater in Buenos Aires where he could be sure of finding what he had really come for, namely treasure.

Having at last decided upon the point of attack the British troops were transferred from the frigates to lighter transports, whilst the *Diadem* and *Diomede* remained anchored near Montevideo, they being too large to proceed up river. On 16 June the transports began to move slowly up the river through the fog and the difficult navigation channels until by the morning of 25 June they had reached Point de Quilmes, eight miles below Buenos Aires.

The Capture of Buenos Aires

Life in Buenos Aires in the year 1806 passed by peacefully. The people went about their business carefully amidst a state of prosperity although it has to be said here, and in Spanish America generally, there was at this time, an undercurrent of revolution stirring in many of the American born inhabitants. It would take too long to take a detailed look at the reasons behind this growing disenchantment with the mother country, but it is fair to say that this was caused by many of the same reasons that caused the North American revolution some thirty years earlier. For example, little opportunity was given to the American born Spaniards, the pick of the government jobs going to Spanish immigrants. Too much of the profit made in South America found its way across the Atlantic instead of being re-invested in the country, and little say was had by many sections of the population in the running of their countries. A general feeling of exploitation and neglect by Spain was rife at the time and this was to manifest itself following the aftermath of the British invasions. But for the time being life was pleasant enough and the days passed by peacefully in stark contrast to those that were about to unfold.

Buenos Aires was the capital city of the Viceroyalty and the seat of the Spanish authorities. It also housed the royal treasury and was the centre of all trade with the interior of the country. The prevailing prosperity had led to an increase in the size of the city. Buenos Aires took the form of a checkerboard with squares set at right angles to each other which formed the streets. The houses were built either of chalk, brick or stone and almost all were of a single storey. Apart from the grand and very fine streets of La Trinidad and San Benito, the streets were the same in appearance and at night were lit by grease lanterns. Most of the houses had a garden at the back and some people had balconies with sun shades and lattice work decorated with flowers and shrubs. One significant feature of the houses was the parapet wall which surrounded the roofs, a feature which will have a great bearing later in our story.

Dominating the city was the Fortress. This served as Government House, Royal Audencia, military headquarters and armoury. It was flanked by bastions and its walls were surrounded by a large, wide ditch. Facing the Fortress on the west was the Plaza Mayor, the main attraction of the city, a large square divided by a building of arcades and sheltered pathways. This building was the Recova, a market place where the city's retailers gathered to do business. To the right of the Fortress stood the Cathedral and nearby was the *Cabildo*, a large colonial building where the Spanish authorities and the local political council had sat and governed since the early days of the settlement. To the north of the city lay an extensive stretch of ground known as the Retiro, upon which were situated the artillery barracks, the arsenal and the Plaza de Toros, or bull-ring. The ground here was higher than the rest of the city and from its elevated position could be seen the isolated monastery of the Recoletas. Finally, on the outskirts of the city there was a large expanse of land set aside for future buildings. This then was Buenos Aires.

Viceroy of the colony was the Marquis de Sobremonte, a man of great political ambition. It was said of him that his temperament:

> ...caused him to seek fortune by the path of false diplomacy, satisfying his own ideas and ambitions by artifice rather than good faith. His best attribute was of a toiler, endowed with intelligence and constructive ability that enabled him to work out his own fortune and contribute to the well being of his fellow countrymen. His administration was honest, a quality greatly to his credit, for ambition is closer to virtue than avarice. [1]

On the afternoon of 24 June 1806, a group of gaucho horsemen rode easily along the banks of the Rio de la Plata, but as they topped a small rise close to the water's edge they suddenly pulled up in astonishment and shock. Whilst a couple of them rode back hastily to the city, the rest of them sat on their horses and gazed out across the river in alarm. Before them lay a British fleet in battle array whilst several hundred British redcoats in small transports glided silently up river.

That same afternoon one of the Marquis de Sobremonte's officers came to him with a report that several British ships had been seen in the river. To Sobremonte, however, this seemed just another vague sighting as he had been receiving such reports since early in the year. He dismissed the report, giving it little credence, adding that the ships were probably smugglers searching the seas for the corsairs *Orion* and *Reina Luisa* from Montevideo. The confident Marquis then put the report out of his mind and returned to his staff, preferring instead to discuss European politics with them.

Even as the British transports groped their way up river the Marquis still continued to attend functions in the normal way completely unaware of the impending threat from the British troops. On the evening of the 24th, he held a reception at his residence to which the leading social and political figures were invited and afterwards they attended a gala performance at the theatre. The hall, 'glittered with profuse extravagance,' oil lamps replacing the old candle-grease lamps, the theatre being brilliantly illuminated by this latest innovation. During the evening, however, an officer came into the royal box and informed Sobremonte that a naval squadron flying the British flag had moored in the river. This time he could not ignore the report or hide his consternation and the news quickly spread to the rest of the alarmed audience. Sobremonte hurried back to the Fortress with his officers as the news spread to the citizens of Buenos Aires who began to prepare themselves for the coming attack.

The British troops disembarked at Point de Quilmes during the afternoon and evening of 25 June and met with no opposition at all, although a hostile force was seen two miles away at the village of Reduction. The troops were transferred into small landing vessels which then proceeded to the shore. However, the water was so shallow that the troops were forced to get into the water and wade knee-deep for about a quarter of a mile to the shore. Captain King, of the navy remained in the water the whole time as a mark for the troops to be guided by, not a pleasant task at all, until the whole of the force had been landed. In all, it consisted of 70 officers and 1571 men, as well as four 6-pounders, two five-and-a-half inch howitzers and two light 3-pounders. As night closed in a steady rain began to fall whilst in the distance fires could be seen burning, as Alexander Gillespie, of the 71st, later wrote,

> Fires were lighted upon every summit, and an immense concourse of horsemen from all directions, to the grand centre of Reduction, a village more than two miles in our front, denoted a general alarm, and that this rising ground was chosen by the enemy as the field for the approaching contest.[2]

In fact, Beresford's force had landed, 'as peaceful as if they were in a desert island before the gaze of the populace'. The people were outraged at the complaisance shown by the authorities and demanded arms and ammunition in order that they might at least show some resistance to the invaders. There was little organisation, however. Each man had his own idea as to what should be done and there was much bravado, each being anxious to display his prowess in the face of the enemy. The few muskets that were kept in the arsenal at the Retiro in Buenos Aires were distributed, though most of the volunteers went without. Midway to Point de Quilmes it was discovered that the ammunition available would not fit the barrels of the muskets anyway and so most of the men marched with swords. The British force, meanwhile, remained under arms throughout the night and waited for the combat they knew would take place the next morning.

At eleven o'clock on the morning of 26 June the British force moved off towards Reduction. They had to cross a level plain which was, for the time being, quite firm and passable even by guns, but which the coming rains would quickly turn into a marshy swamp. Gillespie again:

> Daylight exhibited to us the village of Reduction, nearly two miles on our left, a mass of foot and horse, with four guns upon each flank before us, and a dense column of cavalry hovering upon our right. They were drawn up on the farther extremity of a deep, but verdant morass, and on a chosen flat rising abruptly many yards above our level, like to the steep bank of a river. Nothing could be finer for a defensive position. Early on the morning several of their leaders upon steeds richly caparisoned, and dressed in fine cloaks or ponchos, came down to reconnoitre the borders of the swamp betwixt us, and from their subsequent confidence it may be presumed, that they held our menaces in derision. We had no other alternative but to force our way through every obstacle.[3]

The Spanish force on the heights above Reduction numbered around 3,000, mainly undisciplined cavalry, some even with spears, who presented quite a colourful sight in their bright embroidered cloaks and richly dressed horses. In front of the British lay a deep morass through which the sailors from the ships dragged two 6-pounders. On approaching the enemy Beresford formed the bulk of his men into a single line with the two guns being placed one on each flank, as well as two howitzers in the centre. The St. Helena infantry, with two other guns, were held in reserve to the rear.

The British had not long taken up their position before the Spaniards opened fire. The enemy guns, however, were badly served and most of the shot passed safely overhead. Following this early bombardment a column of infantry began to move upon the British left and on seeing this movement Beresford decided to attack without delay. Orders were given for the whole line to advance, which was promptly and cheerfully obeyed, every man taking off his hat and giving three cheers, the bagpipes of the 71st Regiment striking up at the same time. As it advanced in line to within range of the Spanish guns the small British force was forced to halt in order to enable the guns to pass around the morass which lay in their path. The Spanish guns kept up a stiff fire on the troops who quickened their pace as they advanced. Robert Fernyhough was with the 71st Regiment:

> We had not proceeded far before we got entangled in the morass; which the enemy perceiving, opened a smart fire upon us. Captain le

Blanc, of the seventy-first, unfortunately lost his leg, and underwent immediate amputation on the field. We also had several men killed and wounded; and what added to our difficulties at this moment was that our guns stuck so fast in the morass, that we could not bring one to bear upon the enemy. With some exertion we cleared this impediment, and continued to advance at double-quick time, till we arrived tolerably near when the enemy thought proper to retreat with the utmost precipitation, after receiving two or three volleys of musketry, as well as a brisk cannonading from two brass field pieces, which were fortunately so much to the left of our line that they avoided the morass, and were enabled to gain the heights in time to fire upon the Spaniards as they retreated.[4]

It was indeed easy for Beresford's men who brushed aside the Spaniards with insouciance. After receiving two or three volleys the whole Spanish force was in full flight, abandoning its guns and wagons in disorder. The Spanish commander, Arce, was said to have ordered his men to reform, calling out, 'I gave orders to retreat, not to disband!' and added, 'what will the women of Buenos Aires think of you?'[5]

After halting to extricate their guns from the morass, the British resumed their march upon Reduction. Beresford's next step was to secure the only bridge over the Rio Chuelo, a river about thirty yards wide, which lay about eight miles on from Reduction, barring the way to Buenos Aires. Therefore, he sent forward a small detachment to take it but before they could do so the Spanish defenders set fire to it and it was soon destroyed. Beresford called the detachment back to the main body of the army about a mile from the river where the troops bivouacked for the night. Out in the darkness, meanwhile, the enemy could be heard moving about preparing for the defence of the river crossing the next day.

The dawn of 27 June revealed the Spaniards in a strong position on the opposite bank of the Chuelo protected by hedges and houses and occupying small boats at anchor on the river. The British side of the river was completely devoid of any sort of cover at all. Beresford's first move was to push forward a company of the 71st Regiment who were to get in close under the river bank in order to open fire on the small boats moored there and this was accomplished without any loss. He soon became concerned, however, at the amount of ammunition being expended by the men, there being none nearer to them than that still aboard the British ships and he ordered forward William Gavin, an ensign with the 71st, with a message requesting the men to be more frugal with their fire:

I had to proceed through a plain of upwards of three hundred yards, exposed to the musketry and two field pieces of cannon of the Spaniards, who peppered away at me with the same eagerness as if they had the whole British force before them. I ran in desperation towards my destination, but the bullets whistled so thick about my ears that I thought diverging a little to the right might be safer. When I got into a dyke and proceeded towards my destination, there a six-pound shot came by me (en ricochet). I resumed my old situation on the plain, and arrived under the bank of the river a great deal more frightened than hurt.[6]

Once again the Spanish guns were poorly served and their fire, although heavy, was completely ineffectual doing little damage to the British whose own artillery now came into play. The Spanish guns were sheltered by ditches, hedges and houses but after about an hour they were blasted into silence and the rest of the enemy troops quickly disappeared. The river still had to be crossed, however, but that problem was solved when several seamen swam across to some boats that were fastened to the other side of the river and brought them across to the British side. A bridge was then made over which Beresford's force began to pass with its baggage and equipment, and by eleven o'clock that morning the whole of the British force had crossed the Rio Chuelo, bringing to an end the Spanish resistance. There were now no enemy troops at all between them and Buenos Aires. The way ahead was now open.

As the small but victorious British force advanced unopposed on the city the viceroy, Sobremonte, instead of trying to organise further resistance in the city, decided it was time to make good his escape. He considered any further resistance useless and so, after securing the valuables of the royal treasure, which he sent under escort to the village of Lujan, fifty miles away, he and his family boarded the state coach and travelled with his cavalry to Cordoba where he had been governor some years before. Sobremonte left in charge his aide-de-camp, Hilarion de la Quintana, who advised the people and the militia to assemble in order to accept an honourable surrender. The people protested, however, angry at the treasonable behaviour of the viceroy and at the weak defence put up by their own troops. They said they would rather fight and die than accept surrender and give in tamely. Unfortunately, they could not back up their bold words with bold actions.

Before long a party of British soldiers arrived with a summons for the governor to surrender the city to Beresford and to do so peacefully in order to avoid the bloodshed that would inevitably occur should the people of Buenos Aires decide to resist and fight. At this the people became even more restless and Colonel Ignacio Merle was forced to show himself on the ramparts of the Fortress to tell them that unless the city capitulated within a quarter of an hour they would all be put to the sword. The governor of the city sent an officer with a reply to Beresford requesting some time to draw up conditions but the British commander would have none of it. As Beresford himself later wrote:

I could not consent to delay my march which I had commenced as soon as the whole had crossed the Rio Chuelo; and on arriving near the city an officer of the governor again met me with a number of conditions to which I had not then time to attend, but said I would confirm by writing what I had promised when in possession of the city.[7]

And so, on 27 June 1806, Beresford, at the head of his troops, entered the city of Buenos Aires by the road leading to the church of Santa Domingo and took possession of the Fortress in the centre of the town facing the Plaza Mayor. Alex Gillespie later recalled the scene:

We entered the capital in the afternoon in wide column of order, to give a more imposing show to our little band, amidst a downpour of water, and a very slippery ascent to it. The balconies of the houses were lined with the fair sex, who smiled a welcome, and seemed by no means displeased with the change.[8]

Gillespie mentions here a deception to give the British a show of greater strength. It was a necessary deception that would be used again, although it would not be long before the Spaniards realised just how few British troops there actually were.

Quintana was forced to accept and sign the conditions imposed upon him by Beresford, the main articles being that the garrison was to surrender with all the honours of war and that all commerce and property was to be guaranteed. As soon as the document was signed a salute was fired from the Fortress in honour of His Britannic Majesty's colours being hoisted in South America, and this was answered by Popham's squadron anchored in the river. Buenos Aires was about to begin its brief period of British rule. At a cost of just one man killed and twelve wounded Beresford's force had captured a city of around forty thousand inhabitants along with some 86 pieces of artillery, 550 barrels of gunpowder and hundreds of muskets and swords found in the arsenal. Considering the fact that Beresford's force numbered barely sixteen hundred men the capture of Buenos Aires was indeed quite a remarkable achievement.

For Popham, however, the capture of Buenos Aires was tinged with disappointment, for he soon learned from Quintana that the treasure he had hoped for had been sent away by Sobremonte to Lujan. A party was needed, therefore, to bring the valuables back to the city. The party consisted of thirty-one men of the 71st Regiment and seven dragoons, the whole being placed under the command of Captain Arbuthnot of the 20th Light Dragoons. They left for Lujan on 6 July and in spite of the appalling state of the roads caused by heavy rains they reached the village in three days, returning to the capital on 10 July. They brought back with them over half a million dollars worth of treasure. As well as this amount, a further six hundred thousand dollars were brought in from various other sources such as customs houses, the post office and some private companies. In a despatch dated 16 July, Beresford wrote:

> The sum of one million, eighty-six thousand, two hundred and eight dollars is going home in His Majesty's ship *Narcissus*, and Sir Home Popham and myself thought it right to reserve here, for the exigencies of the army and navy, a considerable sum; and for the purpose of keeping down the exchange drawn on bills drawn by the respective services, and which would otherwise bring the dollar to an enormous price.[9]

A further two hundred thousand dollars were found left behind in the royal treasury so that in all a total of over a million and a quarter dollars were taken by the British. Later, when the prize-money was divided between the principal officers, Sir David Baird received £23,990 5s 8d and Beresford £11,995 2s 10d. Popham, instead of finding himself with a fortune, had to be content with half the amount Beresford had received, which was still not bad, especially when one considers that each soldier and sailor received £18 6s.

After the city had been searched and guards posted in key places Beresford began to install himself in his new headquarters inside the Fortress. He received the city councillors and the military officers who swore allegiance to King George. Along with these came the heads of the churches, the priests and superiors of the convents to add their support. Beresford was anxious to neglect nothing in order to gain their confidence and make the population feel more at ease under British rule. Shops and markets re-opened and trading resumed as normal. Bull-fighting continued at the Plaza de Toros and the inhabitants, as far as possible, returned to their daily routine as before.

The expedition had so far been a great success and yet Beresford and his men were still in a dangerous position. In a way he faced two enemies. There were still some two thousand regular, if poor, troops in the colony as well as about four thousand irregulars and although he could probably hold Buenos Aires itself without cavalry he could never hope to gain control of the whole country. Many of the Spanish troops, as well as a large number of the population, could rise up at the first sign of any weakness and restore Spanish authority to the colony. Conversely, with the viceroy gone there were a great number of the population who wished to capitalise on the situation and rid themselves of Spanish rule. They were not, however, prepared to see a British force in control of the province. It could be said, therefore, that there were two factions in the colony; royalists loyal to Spain and patriots, loyal to the cause of independence. Both had the same objective, namely the overthrow of the British, but at the end of the day they would have different motives. It all made for a very unstable situation in the middle of which Beresford now found himself. The only thing that was certain was that the Spanish people, royalists and patriots alike, wanted to rid themselves of the British.

Nevertheless, for the time being Beresford and Popham were over-joyed at the success of their expedition. In fact, Popham even took the unprecedented step of sending home to England a circular to the leading merchants in London announcing new and lucrative markets which he had opened up to them. He thought this news would be welcomed with jubilation by British commerce as it would make a mockery of Napoleon's plan to exclude Britain from trade with the rest of Europe, his plan being to try and starve her into submission. With the markets of South America opened up to them Britain's merchants and businessmen need not worry any more. Beresford, on the other hand, was more concerned with rela-tions with the colonists. Without any official orders he would just have to use his own discretion in all matters.

But even as the British began to settle down in Buenos Aires, the reper-cussions of the invasion were just beginning to be felt in London. At the end of July the letters written by both Beresford and Popham whilst at St. Helena reached London. Needless to say the government were none too pleased, for they found themselves in a difficult position. The expedition had been carried out without either their knowledge or sanction and with such scant information at hand they could do no more than send instruc-tions to Beresford to the effect that he was to try and hold his position and have as little contact as possible with the local population.

In particular, he was to avoid at all costs any involvement in any 'revo-lutionary enterprises', a possible reference to Popham's known sympa-thies with patriotic causes. If he found the situation too difficult he was to return immediately with his men to the Cape. In the meantime, a force of about 3,000 men, under Sir Samuel Auchmuty, would be despatched to the Rio de la Plata.

At Cape Colony, meanwhile, Sir David Baird had also received a letter from Beresford, written as soon as the latter had occupied Buenos Aires. Baird replied immediately, offering his congratulations and adding that he was sending to the Rio de la Plata a further reinforcement of 2,000 men which was to sail on 29 August. This reinforcement, under Lieutenant-Colonel Backhouse, of the 47th Regiment, was much needed by Beresford in Buenos Aires for no matter how many ruses were employed by the British in an attempt to deceive the Spaniards it soon became apparent to the inhabitants that the strength of the British force was nowhere near as great as had originally been thought. A passage from the diary of William Gavin illustrates a typical encounter between the British soldier and the Spaniards:

The Spaniards soon discovered our strength by the rations daily drawn. I was accosted one day by an inhabitant who enquired as to our numbers, which I exaggerated some hundreds, when he very impertinently asked 'how were they fed as rations were only issued for such a number'. I accounted for it as men in hospital, servants, etc. but it would not do, they knew to a man our strength.[10]

As a result of this discovery a great sense of shame overcame the people and along with it arose a great desire to rise up and rid themselves of the invaders. Alex Gillespie recalled an incident which happened whilst he and some others were drinking at a tavern called *Los Tres Reyes*:

At the same table sat many Spanish officers, with whom, a few hours before, we had combated, who had become prisoners by the capture of the city, and were regaling upon the suave fare with ourselves. A handsome young woman served both parties, but on her brow sat a deep frown.[11]

Gillespie naturally thought her displeasure was aimed at him and his comrades and asked the young woman for an explanation. He went on:

After thanking us for this honourable declaration she instantly turned to her countrymen, who were at the other end of a long table; addressing herself to them in a loud and impressive tone. 'I wish that you gentlemen had informed us sooner of your cowardly intentions to surrender Buenos Aires, for I will stake my life that had we known it the women would have turned out unanimously, and driven back the English with stones.'[12]

Nevertheless, the small British force remained in Buenos Aires in peace, be it an uneasy one, until the end of July, when they began to get a little suspicious of things in the city and soon the whole atmosphere there began to change. Attempts were made by the people to lure the troops into the countryside, sentries were set upon or kidnapped, the German mercenaries, recruited in Cape Colony, deserted and numerous other plots were hatched by the people.

One soldier of the 71st happened to be cleaning his musket one day in one of the barrack rooms and when he went to stick his ramrod into the floor it suddenly disappeared. Whilst searching for it the man discovered that the whole of the barracks had been mined from the other side of the street where there was, of all things, a convent of friars. Further examination revealed that some hard work had gone into digging the mine and that some barrels of gunpowder had actually been placed in position beneath the barracks. Had they not been discovered, the explosives would, sooner or later, have blown the British troops to atoms. Alex Gillespie also mentioned this plot and added that thirty-six barrels of powder were to have been used to blow up the barracks used by the 71st.

At the head of the instigators of these plots were the men of the Church, the Catholic priests and bishops, who from their pulpits openly incited the people to rise up and rid themselves of the heretic invaders. These men of the church showed great friendship and respect to Beresford one minute, but the next were openly plotting against him. In his journal Captain Pococke, also of the 71st, wrote with increasing concern of the prevailing atmosphere in Buenos Aires. His entry for Saturday, 19 July 1806, reads:

> The Spaniards are doing all in their power to encourage our men to desert our service, and go into the country and join their own. Several have been detected in the act. This looks like a cloud hanging over our heads and which one day or other will burst.[13]

Pococke's journal contains almost daily reports of the various rumours that were circulating, of the inhabitants' intentions to rise up, and of the need for the garrison to be on its guard, ready to turn out at a moment's notice.

Things came to a head towards the end of July when Beresford received information that an armed force of Spaniards had gathered and was planning to attack the city. This force had been gathered together by the 29 year-old Juan Martin de Pueyrredon, born in the province and the son of a Frenchman who had become a naturalised Spaniard. Together with his younger brothers, Pueyrredon planned to recruit one thousand horsemen as the basis for a force with which he hoped to recapture the city, and in this he was greatly assisted by a rich Spanish merchant, Martin de Alzaga, as well as other patriots. The inhabitants, too, prepared themselves for the rising. Arms were hidden in the city and made ready, and each night Pueyrredon's followers met in secret to receive his instructions. When all was ready his force assembled at Cacerios de Perdriel, about ten miles from Buenos Aires.

Beresford, however, had learned of the impending attack and decided to march out and meet the Spaniards in the field. Early on the morning of 1 August he duly marched out of the city with 500 men of the 71st Regiment, fifty men of the St. Helena Regiment and twelve guns. They marched in silence across the open countryside until at about eight o'clock that morning the enemy was sighted. Unfortunately for Beresford, his guide had taken the wrong route which took the British the long way round, by which time the Spanish outposts had alerted the main camp.

The Spaniards were drawn up behind a stone wall with a battery of four guns and two *pedros*, small guns which fired stone balls. These were under the command of a Captain Trellis who had with him twenty-four gunners along with an infantry escort of twenty men on either flank. Pueyrredon's men fell in behind the guns, to the rear of which were a number of mounted *blandengoes*. On getting within range Beresford put his guns in the centre and charged both flanks with his infantry. He wrote later:

> There appeared about 2,000, chiefly cavalry. My men were so anxious to approach the enemy that I immediately formed my disposition for the attack and proceeded to it. The enemy frequently cheered as we approached.[14]

The British troops had advanced to within about a thousand yards when the Spaniards opened fire with their guns. As usual they were poorly served and badly aimed and little damage was done. It was then time for the British guns to reply. Thomas Pococke described the action:

> After firing seven or eight rounds at them they faced to their right and left and filed off, as if to leave the field. Those who faced to their right came close to galloping across our left flank, near which were posted two howitzers, and immediately that they got clear of the flank they wheeled short round to our rear, but in the most irregular manner possible, and about five of them were mad enough to make a dash at one of our ammunition carts, which was bringing up the rear quite unprotected being only loaded with grain for the mules, which they succeeded in carrying off, and desperately wounding one of the drivers with a sword in several places. One of his legs was instantly amputated. Our light infantry faced about, then dashed after them, but could not save the fellow.[15]

The *gauchos* charged again making straight for Beresford who had become separated from his staff. To his horror he found that the rain had rusted his sword in its scabbard and was stuck fast. Captain Arbuthnot managed to keep one of them at bay but another carried on until Lieutenant Mitchell ordered some grenadiers to fire at him, bringing both horse and rider crashing to the ground. Pueyrredon, too, had his horse shot beneath him by a piquet of the 71st. He landed on his feet grasping his flag crying, 'vive la patrie', and expecting to die at any moment, when suddenly one of his *gauchos*, named Lorenzo, came charging up and Pueyrredon was able to save himself by vaulting up behind him into the saddle.

Beresford's men soon scattered the rest of the Spaniards and they were left in possession of four 8-pounders, five 2-pounders and one destroyed 18-pounder, as well as pistols, muskets and ammunition. Eighteen prisoners were also captured. The British casualties numbered just three wounded but as Pococke wrote:

The killed and wounded of the enemy must have been considerable, but all except a few were carried off the field. We observed them fastening the person (dead) to the horse's saddle with a rope which they carry to catch horses, and they galloped off as hard as they could.[16]

That same evening the British troops marched back in triumph to Buenos Aires which they reached at about five o'clock, by which time large crowds had gathered to see them return. Several rumours had spread amongst the people, one being that Beresford's men had been cut to pieces. The appearance of the British, therefore, dampened their spirits and only served to heighten the tension further. As Pococke wrote in his journal:

I am inclined to think that from this day we shall be in continual hot water with them, and that it has been the commencement of what is to follow the first favourable opportunity. God grant that we may receive a reinforcement to enable us to put a final check to their proceedings. [17]

Unfortunately, for Beresford and his small British force this wish was not to be granted.

III

La Reconquista

The defeat of Pueyrredon and his cavalry at Perdriel had given Beresford some breathing space, and for the time being he thought himself safe from further attack until the arrival of British reinforcements. But even during this moment of respite there was, across the waters of the Rio de la Plata, a much larger force on the move against him. As early as mid-July this force had been gathering in Montevideo, arming itself in preparation for a counter-attack on Buenos Aires.

The leader of this force was Santiago Liniers, a 53-year old French émigré who had lived in the country for thirty years having entered the service of Spain, and who had risen to a high rank in the Spanish navy. He was a man full of spirit and ambition and had established important relationships and contacts throughout society as a result of his marriage to the daughter of a rich and powerful merchant, Martin de Saratea. At the time of Beresford's invasion Liniers was stationed at Ensenada and was in charge of the coastal defences there. Of the few officers of rank in Buenos Aires, Santiago Liniers was the most capable to lead the reconquest of the city.

Liniers arrived in the Buenos Aires during the British invasion and went to his father-in-law's house. There, he was told by his friends of the plan to retake the city, as they needed a force to serve as the basis for their operations it was decided that Liniers should go to Montevideo and appeal to the governor, Ruiz Huidobro, for help.

Accordingly, at the beginning of July, he set out from Las Conchas and sailed for Colonia. Having arrived in Montevideo Liniers offered his services to Huidobro and said that he was willing to take command of any expedition against the British in Buenos Aires. The offer was accepted as Huidobro also saw it as a chance to rid Montevideo of Popham's ships, which were blockading the city.

The people of Montevideo rallied to Liniers' cause. Volunteers from all parts of the colony were assembled and arms and supplies gathered together in stores. The nucleus of Liniers' force that was to march against the British in Buenos Aires consisted of about eight hundred regular troops from the remaining regular regiments, the Regimiento de Infanteria de Buenos Aires, the Regimiento de Dragones de Buenos Aires, the Regimiento de Blandengoes de Buenos Aires, the Real Cuerpo de Artilleria and the Batallon de Voluntarios de Infanteria de Montevideo. There were also a further one hundred and forty men from riding clubs as well as some mercenaries. Along with these a further five hundred volunteers joined the expedition, and on 22 July the 1,300-strong force left Montevideo.

By 1 August, Liniers' men had reached Colonia where they were joined by six officers and a hundred men of the Regimiento de Voluntarios de Caballeria de la Colonia, under the command of Captains Pedro Manuel Garcia and Benito Chain. These two companies had been sent by Huidobro to strengthen the force and soon they were all embarked in the various ships, schooners, gun-boats and merchantmen that were to transport them across the Rio de la Plata to the opposite shore and Buenos Aires.

That same day there arose a violent storm which delayed Liniers' passage across the river but by a twist of fate this storm was to prove a great ally to him. On the night of 3 August Liniers put to sea and, aided by the same storm that had delayed him, managed to cross the river. This hurricane force wind was known as the *pampero*, a strong wind which blows from the Cordillera de los Andes, across the plains of the pampas that lie to the north of Buenos Aires. Coming across this plain it gathers enormous strength until by the time it reaches the waters of the Rio de la Plata it is mighty enough to create huge waves. Fortunately for Liniers, it helped him cross unseen and he landed safely at Las Conchas, thirty miles north of Buenos Aires. Not so lucky, however, were the British ships patrolling the river. Many were badly damaged in the storm or crippled and were unable to find or stop Liniers who went undetected.

At Las Conchas, Liniers found fresh food and supplies but most important of all, he found volunteers. Armed patriotic supporters had turned out in great numbers to meet him and join his army. All shared his determination to take back their capital from the British invaders. Amongst them was Pueyrredon, defeated by Beresford at Perdriel but still full of determination, again bringing with him his gaucho horsemen. A great many other volunteer groups turned out with their leaders as well as many individuals, some on foot but mainly mounted on their own horses, giving them a distinct advantage over the British as mounted troops were the only ones capable of negotiating the difficult and swampy countryside.

Meanwhile, on board the *Diadem* Popham was still feeling quite pleased with himself having taken Buenos Aires and its treasure. On hearing of

Liniers' sudden and successful crossing of the river he did not seem unduly alarmed or worried for Beresford, to whom he wrote on 5 August:

> Early in the morning, I have been informed by Captain Thompson that under the storm of the preceding day Liniers had crossed from Colonia completely unobserved by our ships, passing by Las Palmas without being obliged to use the canal…when the enemy gives you a good opportunity to show your bravery I trust that you will destroy four times more their number when you display your troops, and I hope you find a good place to perform your work. According to the description received about the capacity of Liniers' vessels, I cannot believe they convey more than a thousand men. [1]

Popham may not have been too far off the mark in estimating the number of troops aboard Liniers' ships, but he could not know that many more were waiting at Las Conchas and that others had joined and were still joining since. Captain Pococke, of the 71st, certainly did not share Popham's confidence:

> Everything tends to evince to us the near approach of the enemy, and that in a few days we shall be attacked by them; and if they hold unanimously together there can be no doubt whatever of the result. What with soldiers of all descriptions, joined with all the inhabitants, it is impossible that we can for any time withstand them. [2]

Between the 6th and 8th of August the rain fell in such torrents that the roads were quickly turned into quagmires. They became totally impassable to the British, depriving Beresford of a chance to march out again and meet the Spaniards in the field.

The latter, on the other hand, had no problem crossing the countryside, mounted as most of them were on horses. The bad weather continued and whilst the British troops spent their time preparing to deal with any possible attack, the people of Buenos Aires pressed on with their own preparations knowing that Liniers' army would shortly be poised to strike out against the city. They grew increasingly bold, continually harassing the British sentries posted throughout the city, and attacking the patrols sent out into the streets.

> …one of the sentries was knocked down at his post. The officer of the guard came to his assistance, and was stabbed in the back most dangerously. The man who committed this outrage was immediately seized, after receiving several bayonets in the body.[3]

And this from Pococke:

About 10pm four Spaniards surrounded one of our sentries at the tobacco stores, and took his firelock from him. There was no great courage in doing so, as he was only a boy of sixteen years of age – a marine. [4]

The situation in the city deteriorated seriously until Beresford decided it was time to evacuate the sick and wounded to Ensenada. But once again the bad weather prevented him from acting and he was forced to postpone the operation, earmarking 12 August as a new date. By then, however, it would be too late.

By 10 August Liniers' army had reached the outskirts of the city and with such an overwhelming numerical advantage he felt sure Beresford would surrender. Accordingly, he sent forward his aide, Hilarion de la Quintana, with an ultimatum summoning him to do so. Quintana, however, found the British commander in conference and in no mood to entertain any such ultimatum. But as Quintana threatened to leave Beresford finally took it from him.

The letter from Liniers recalled how Beresford had entered Buenos Aires in an audacious manner with a small number of troops to assail a large population which, he pointed out, was lost by lack of direction. Now, however, the people were full of patriotic enthusiasm and were willing to show further proof of their bravery. He then went on to point out the fact that he was now advancing with regular troops, superior to the British, and that he demanded unconditional surrender immediately. Beresford's reply to the ultimatum was as follows:

I am in possession of your note, and I agree that the fortunes of arms vary: I do not doubt that you have superiority in number but the comparison of discipline is useless. On this knowledge I say that I will defend as long as I feel it prudent to do so, to avoid the calamity that can fall upon this population, that none more than myself will regret. [5]

Beresford was indeed quite correct in stating that his own troops were superior to Liniers' in discipline, but unless they could meet the Spaniards in the field this would count for little. As it turned out the Spanish army would penetrate the city and force Beresford's men to fight in the streets and on the rooftops. Under such conditions, command would prove difficult with units scattered throughout the streets. Moreover, the traditional British method of fighting would be impossible to employ, and thus the advantage would lie with Liniers' men. Despite the majority of them being little more than an armed mob, there were more than enough regular and irregular troops under Liniers to give the Spaniards the advantage, particularly as the nature of the fighting would be close quarter street fighting.

Having received Beresford's reply Liniers was left with no choice but to use force to retake the city, and accordingly he ordered his men forward into positions ready for the attack. Liniers moved his men forward by the left to the north of the city, and by evening they were in position around the Retiro where a small British guard was posted. Robert Fernyhough wrote:

> The enemy advanced that night as far as the park [the Retiro], where we had a guard consisting of a sergeant, corporal, and twenty privates, who, all excepting two, were put to death in a shocking manner, their bodies being cut and mangled and afterwards thrown naked on the beach. We had several skirmishes during the night, in which Captain Ogilvie, of the artillery and several of the men were wounded.[6]

Indeed, the Spanish troops at the Retiro were now in great strength and they commenced a steady firing on the British which grew heavier during the night. The people of Buenos Aires, realising Liniers' attack had begun, also began firing from the windows of their homes and soon a galling fire had opened up from all around the Retiro, causing the British to pull back and take cover, standing at arms throughout the rest of the night.

11 August began quietly until at about three in the morning the tension was broken by Beresford who launched a counter-attack. The 71st Regiment was divided into three parties, under Pack, Major Toley, and Colonel Campbell respectively. Toley's party was to advance along the riverside to engage the enemy whilst Pack and Campbell took another route in order to take the Spaniards in the flank and rear. The attack got underway with the British troops stealing silently forward through the gloomy streets but the Spaniards were much too alert and with the people everywhere up in arms it was impossible to achieve any element of surprise. The British troops did their best but were beaten back with some loss as the Spaniards advanced deeper into the city. Thomas Pococke described the fighting of 11 August:

> About an hour after daylight a heavy firing of musketry commenced from the people concealed in the houses, as also from the tops of them – most of which were constructed in the manner as popular parapets to fire over – on our piquets and sentries, who were not tardy in returning it. Several of our men were wounded, as also, no doubt, many on the side of the enemy. About 11am the enemy commenced firing with a heavy gun at the *Iasthma* (lying close to the shore); but luckily she had prepared to do her duty, and after firing a great number at her without effect, a shot struck her somewhere about her mizzen-graft, and instantly down dropped the English

ensign. I hope such was not ominous of their future success. This occasioned a great huzzah from the enemy; but Jack did not keep them in suspense, for the colours were soon up again. The ship fired with great energy and activity, as also did two gunboats. The enemy, after about an hour's employment in this way, ceased firing at her, so it is supposed some accident befell their gun, or that the vessels committed destruction either among the people or their houses. The enemy kept up this annoying fire from the houses until dark. [7]

The skirmishing continued until nightfall with casualties being suffered on both sides, and when the firing stopped Liniers' men moved forward a little more to take up their positions for the main attack the next day. By now almost the whole population of Buenos Aires had turned out to support Liniers, and with such an immense force facing him Beresford decided that the best way of trying to hold off the Spaniards would be to concentrate his men. Thus, he pulled all of them back into the Plaza Mayor and into the high buildings surrounding it. From here they could be supported by the guns in the Fortress.

The Plaza Mayor, or main square, was divided by a long colonnaded building called the Recova, inside which was the 71st Regiment with the St. Helena infantry posted in a position to enfilade the rear entrances. The marines and the seamen were drawn up in front and guns brought up to cover the approaches on the flanks. The main houses around the square were also occupied. The British troops took up their positions and Beresford could do no more than wait for daylight and the Spanish attack whilst here and there out in the night could be heard the odd crackle of musketry from the excited Spanish masses.

Liniers, meanwhile, had formed his plan of attack, although in the circumstances, that is to say the confined spaces of the streets, it would have to be a simple one. Tactics in the normal sense of the word would be impossible. It would simply be a case of pushing as many men as possible against the British and hoping for the best. In spite of the conditions, Liniers intended to try and control the attack as best he could. He decided to divide his men into three columns with himself taking command of the first whilst Gutierrez de la Concha and Colonel Pinedo took the second and third respectively. Liniers' men, along with the second column, were to attack the Plaza Mayor whilst Pinedo's column would cut off any retreat the British might make away from the square.

By daybreak on 12 August a fog had settled in Buenos Aires and taking advantage of it some Spanish *Minones*, light irregular troops, started their attack early on their own initiative, attacking down the Calle del Cabildo. They opened up a steady fire on the British sentries posted in front of the Plaza. Once this attack had started more Spaniards moved in to support them and soon the musketry became heavy on all sides At about 9 o'clock more of Liniers' men charged off from the Retiro, again without orders, and the Spaniards' commander, realising that his army was already virtually beyond his control, ordered the main attack to begin.

The British troops returned the Spaniards' fire but it soon became apparent that the enemy had occupied most of the houses around the Plaza and also some churches after forcing out the British troops that had been positioned there. The pressure became so great on Beresford's men that he gave orders for his guns to open fire, showering the enemy with shells and grape-shot that wrecked havoc in the confined spaces of the narrow streets. The main Spanish attack was now in progress and British soldiers were falling fast, not only without being able to get to grips with the enemy, as they usually would in battle, but without even seeing them either. The Spaniards had kept up a galling fire from the tops of the convents and churches that commanded the Plaza and Fortress, and a similarly damaging fire was directed at the British from the tops of the houses. These houses, as already stated, were built with parapets around the roofs which in turn communicated with each other and the enemy marksmen were able to take aim and fire without exposing themselves to much danger.

The Spanish attack developed almost as Liniers had planned except that Pinedo advanced along the Calle La Catedral and De la Concha along the Calle San Jose. The attack was quite disorganised with the crowds of people mixing with the different regular and militia units. But it was also effective, with the encirclement of the Plaza being achieved without too much trouble. Robert Fernyhough was in the thick of the action:

> Towards the middle of the day our men began to fall very fast, particularly those at the guns. They were picked off from the tops of the houses, which were occupied by the enemy, who kept up such an incessant fire of musketry, that it became impossible for the men to stand to their guns. We lost three officers almost at the same time. One was Captain Kennet, of the Royal Engineers, he was shot dead by the General's side. [8]

Liniers' artillery had now entered the fray also. The people that had joined the assault had pushed an 18-pounder and a mortar along the Calle Las Torres, there were two 4-pounders in Del Cabildo, another 18-pounder and a mortar in the Calle La Merced al Norte and a 4-pounder in La Catedral. Liniers' infantry had occupied the blocks of houses along the Calles San Jose, San Carlos and La Pieded and from these they could command the roofs of the mansion house, cathedral and the other houses around the Plaza Mayor, as could the Spanish troops who opened fire from the church towers of St. Francis and St. Ignatius.

Time and time again Pueyrredon's cavalry charged into the Plaza in an attempt to carry away the British guns but were driven back with loss, and the city's inhabitants, by now inextricably mixed with the regular troops, repeatedly advanced to the attack, pushed forwards by the sheer weight of their own numbers behind them. These crowds, however, were an easy target for the British infantry who cut them down in droves with a storm of musketry and grape. In spite of their overwhelming numerical superiority their attacks were repulsed by the British troops on the roof of the Recova and in the Cabildo, as well as those steadfastly hanging on to their positions in the cathedral. However, it was only a matter of time before the masses broke through to the main British position. The deciding factor was the heavy fire being poured down on Beresford's men from the rooftops around them, for when this began to take its toll the tide gradually turned in Liniers' favour. 'This unremitting fire,' wrote Pococke,

> ...continued from every direction till about one o'clock when I observed the General (who was walking under a wall near my company) to be extremely agitated at beholding so many fine fellows carried into the fort killed and wounded, and at this time there was not a church or house which could in the smallest degree command the market square but was filled with men who were enabled to take deliberate aim, being perfectly secure from our fire. Great numbers of artillery fell, and one or two of the guns were obliged to be manned by the men. [9]

The British troops in the cathedral still clung to their position, but they soon came under heavy pressure from Gutierrez de la Concha and his volunteers until gradually they were forced out. The 71st Regiment, too, were forced back from the arches of the Recova, disputing every yard, leaving the ground strewn with the bodies of their dead and dying comrades, but leaving an even greater number of Spaniards dead in the streets approaching the Plaza. On seeing the 71st retreating, Pueyrredon, who was positioned nearby with his cavalry, charged them and captured a pipe banner from one of the pipers.

It soon became clear to Beresford that with such heavy odds stacked against him it would be impossible to hold on to the Plaza Mayor any longer and at about two o'clock in the afternoon he ordered all of his men back inside the Fortress. There followed an almighty scramble as the harassed British soldiers withdrew to the Fort, the wounded being either helped back by their comrades or dragging themselves to safety whilst musket balls whizzed all around them. Beresford himself was the last to cross before the drawbridge was raised. All the effective British troops were now inside the Fortress and having lost 165 men, and not wishing to lose any more in what was now obviously a losing battle, Beresford was left with no other choice but to lower the Union Jack and raise a white flag of truce.

No sooner had the British troops raised the white flag than it was reported to Liniers by Lieutenant Baptiste Raymond, and he ordered Quintana forward to see what Beresford wanted. However, whether it was difficult to see the white flag through the smoke of battle is not clear but the Spaniards continued firing until they saw Quintana and Raymond enter the Fortress. At this the Spaniards surged forward from their positions, completely out of control, leaving the British troops inside in a state of some anxiety:

> Instantly, as the gate was closed and the bridge drawn up, the enemy sallied forth from their lurking places and the whole square from the Cabildo to the Fortress was crowded with their soldiers, of all descriptions and such a rabble as I have never seen before and I hope I never shall see again. [10]

Robert Fernyhough, with the 71st, also recorded the events:

> Never shall I forget the scene which followed the hoisting of the flag of truce, and the advantage gained over us; about 4000 ragamuffins rushed into the square, brandishing their knives, threatening us with destruction. The savages paid no regard to our flag of truce, and were firing in all directions. [11]

Having seen Quintana enter the Fortress with the parlementary drum, the Spaniards surged forward to its walls. Liniers and his officers had to threaten them in order to hold them back and it was only with great difficulty that he made them realise that the Fortress had not yet surrendered and that the white flag might be only be in order to ask for a suspension of hostilities. He later admitted that Beresford, had he wished to do so, could have taken advantage of the situation by pulling down the flag and opening fire. He would then have had a regular massacre on his hands. Liniers also said that whilst this would still not have been sufficient to take the final victory from him it would, nevertheless, have been more bloodily achieved.

Eventually enough order was restored to allow Quintana to parley with Beresford. Liniers' aide was introduced to Beresford by another English officer. He asked Beresford what his intentions were, adding that Liniers would not accept conditional surrender but simply wanted the British to throw down their arms, in which case he would guarantee their safety. The British troops themselves were by now showing signs of fear owing to the increased clamouring of the mob outside the Fortress. Quintana, therefore, gave more assurances and went with Beresford to the wall above the entrance to the Fort. From there Quintana addressed the crowd, and told them to leave the square and await Liniers' arrival. The crowd, however, were unappeased and demanded the British general's sword. Beresford unsheathed it and offered it to Quintana who twice refused it, saying that Liniers should be the one to accept it. At this refusal an English officer took it from Beresford and threw it into the crowd hoping the gesture would calm them down. At the foot of the wall was a Spanish officer, Captain Hipolito Mordeile, who picked it up and took it back to Beresford.

The crowd were growing more and more restless and Quintana was once again forced to appeal for calm, but it seemed that they would only do so when the Spanish flag was raised. Fortunately, a British sailor managed to find one, perhaps the one that had flown above the Fortress before the Union Jack took its place. But still Beresford feared for the safety of his men. At this point Gutierrez de la Concha stepped forward saying that he would guarantee the lives of the British soldiers, adding that if anyone approached them or did any harm to them in any way they would pay for it with their life. For a while it seemed as though he would have to be as good as his word, for the rabble clamoured forward shouting, 'cutchileo,' meaning that they wanted to kill the British on the spot.

At length a Spanish flag was hoisted above the Fortress and as the crowd began cheering a line of regular infantry marched forward and some calm was restored. Quintana could now see that Liniers was approaching and he asked Beresford whether he would prefer to see him inside the Fortress or out in the Plaza. Beresford decided upon the latter and together with de la Concha and Mordeile he marched out to meet Liniers who embraced him and apologised for the behaviour of his men which he said was owing to their ignorance of the rules of war. Verbal terms were then agreed by the two men, to be ratified later, the main points being that the British hand over the Fortress and march out with all the honours of war and give up their arms.

Meanwhile, Beresford returned to his men and made a short speech to them, praising their gallantry. Then, with the 71st leading the way with colours unfurled, they marched out between two files of Spanish infantry. The officers signed a parole book and were allowed to keep their swords whilst the men grounded their arms before being taken to various places as prisoners of war. The colours of the 71st were also surrendered, the ceremony taking place before men who were already angered at the outcome of the fight. To see one's regimental colours lost in battle was bad enough, but to see them simply surrendered to the enemy was worse, and this only increased the distress of the British soldiers further, as Robert Fernyhough recalled:

> The poor fellows were in the greatest state of excitement, and bitterly lamented not being allowed to continue the action. Some of them, with tears in their eyes, requested most earnestly to be permitted to die with arms in their hands. I believe a set of men were never more

ready to sacrifice their lives for King and country, than the brave men who composed our little army on that day.[12]

The fighting was over, for the time being at least, and the British troops were marched off into prison whilst Liniers gave instructions for Beresford and his staff to be lodged in the house of Felix Casamayor, one of the city's wealthiest men. The wounded British soldiers were taken to the hospital at the Residencia where they were treated by their own surgeons, and when everything had at last settled down to a relatively calm state the Spaniards could congratulate themselves not only on the recapture of their capital but arms and trophies taken from the British. These included six flags, four mortars and twenty-six guns, and around 1,400 prisoners.

Beresford himself felt greatest disappointment at his failure to hold Buenos Aires. He was also most anxious to see that no harm came to his men who were likewise in a distressed state and very downhearted at their failure. He realised, however, that he could minimize the extent of his failure in the eyes of the British public if he could secure a satisfactory form of capitulation. He discussed the possibilities of this with Casamayor, who then visited Liniers at his private residence. The two discussed Beresford's views and Casamayor suggested to Liniers a capitulation which would be acceptable to both generals and would look good in the eyes of both the Spanish colonists and the British government. The same afternoon, 13 August, Beresford met Liniers at the Fortress to discuss the terms, and several meetings later the general produced his proposals. Beresford translated them verbally as neither Casamayor nor Liniers were able to speak English.

> I had a fair copy, which was read over and translated to him [Liniers], paragraph by paragraph, in presence of Lieutenant-Colonel Pack and Senor Casamayor. Senor Liniers was extremely anxious with me to make some alterations in our original agreement, but which in one case I refused, and he finally, on signing this paper, took it and gave it to his friend Casamayor, desiring him to get it translated, and to see that it was such as they understood it, making the alteration I had agreed to.[13]

Liniers made some alterations to Beresford's proposals but he was in a difficult position. He was a greater admirer of the British general's character and wished to be as generous as possible to him, but he also had his duty to the Spanish people, of course, and had to secure terms which would be acceptable to them. Eventually, Liniers signed the document, placing the word, *concedido*, meaning conceded, before his name. The document was dated 12 August 1806, and there were five main points.

First, that all British prisoners were to be embarked as soon as possible on board the British transports moored in the river, and then conveyed to the dominions of His Britannic Majesty. Second, it was agreed that all Spanish prisoners taken by Beresford would be exchanged for the British prisoners, and that the British transports leaving the colony would be guaranteed protection against attack on the voyage home. Third, that provisions would be supplied for the voyage. Fourth, such wounded of the British troops as could not be moved would remain in Buenos Aires in hospitals in the care of either British or Spanish surgeons, and that on their recovery they too would be sent home. Finally, the property of all British subjects in Buenos Aires was to be respected. The document of surrender being signed, Beresford and his men could look forward to a short wait before being re-embarked in British ships in order to return to either Britain or one of her possessions. That was the theory. In practice, however, it became quite a different story.

The people of Buenos Aires were still celebrating their victory and had become intoxicated with their success. Before long, however, they heard the news that the Marquis de Sobremonte would shortly be returning to restore his rule to the colony. Needless to say, this news was greeted with derision by the people and a sense of defiance set in amongst them. After all, they had just overpowered a British force and had become very conscious of their own power. They were certainly in no mood to accept the return of the unpopular viceroy. Their victory brought about a great shift to the political climate of the colony. The old military command was discredited along with Sobremonte and the excited populace looked amongst themselves for a new leader.

With the rumours of British reinforcements on their way to the Rio de la Plata the people once again looked to Santiago Liniers to repel this new threat. They proclaimed him as their leader in opposition to the Cabildo who saw him as a menace and a threat to their power. Therefore, the Cabildo called a council of the civil and ecclesiastical authorities, as was the custom under Spanish rule, in order to avoid a confrontation with the people, at the head of whom were men of a younger and more cultured generation.

These men were imbued with the ideas of freedom and European Enlightenment, and the fall of Sobremonte acted as a signal for them to take the first steps down the long road to independence from Spain. The crowd of people at the meeting would not obey their Spanish leaders and again shouted Liniers' name. They invaded the Assembly Hall and demanded the Cabildo to bow to their demands, to expel Sobremonte from Buenos Aires and to install Liniers as military commander. As one Argentine historian later put it:

> This was the first manifestation of the people's sovereignty and had a direct bearing on future political events, awakening the colonial inhabitants to a national aspiration for a free, and independent nation.[14]

The Cabildo still remained in opposition to Liniers. At the head of these Spanish leaders was Martin de Alzaga, who saw in Liniers a lack of will power, mainly because of the latter's acceptance of Beresford's terms of surrender. The people too, although proclaiming Liniers as their leader, were against the terms of the treaty. In particular, they were strongly against the clause which would allow the British prisoners to re-embark and sail away as soon as possible because it was now widely believed that British reinforcements were on their way and the people wanted to hold the prisoners as hostages. This placed Liniers in a difficult position and he realised that if he was to maintain his popularity with the people he would have to go back on certain promises made to Beresford.

Consequently, on 18 August, when Liniers received the official Spanish translation of the terms for his signature, realising his generous concessions, and not wishing to betray the people, he added to the word, '*concedido*,' the words, '*en quanto puedo*', which meant, 'conceded as far as I am able to do so.' Needless to say, when Beresford received the document he immediately submitted a strong letter of protest to Liniers, dated 21 August, in which he expressed great astonishment at the addition of the words, '*en quanto puedo*'.

The British commander wrote a number of times to Liniers but as his letters went unanswered he assumed he was being ignored. He also tried, in vain, to see Liniers personally in order to make the final preparations for the re-embarkation of his men under the terms of the capitulation, which he assumed were still valid. Liniers promised to call upon the British commander to make these arrangements, his assurance being given daily, until on 26 August the two finally met at Liniers' house. Beresford had with him his aide-de-camp, Captain Arbuthnot, and he described the meeting as follows:

As soon as we were seated, with a great deal of apparent sensibility and declared regret, Senor Liniers for the first time communicated to me that the British troops were to be detained, and he so fully launched out in condemnation of the breach of faith towards us, and the infamy of the transaction, declaring his own inability to resist or prevent it, that I had nothing to add, but merely said the only thing under such circumstances that remained for me was to protest, to which he immediately answered that I certainly ought and he would second it. I remarked on the addition he had put to his signature to the English and Spanish copies of the capitulation, which he endeavoured to explain as being of the same validity as if without it. On the same evening of that day about dark he sent his aide-de-camp to inform me of his resolution to embark our people, but as the people of the town were against it and in a state of insurrection it would be necessary to do it privately and requested for that purpose that I would order the transport to a certain place out of sight of the town, and that he would prepare all the small craft and continue to send our men off in the night time. As nothing was done I conclude that the adverse party to this proceeding had got wind of it, as I understood that late in the evening of this day, or in the morning a deputation from that function waited on him, and informed him that if he had further communication with me he would be considered as a suspected person, and other means, one of which (an accusation of bribery against him) he states in his letter frightened him into whatever measures they saw fit, and first obliging him to deny what he had put his signature to.[15]

The outcome was that although Liniers had intended to re-embark Beresford and his men, the circumstances and popular opinion prevented him from doing so. The treaty was thus rendered meaningless. Another significant result of the whole episode was that Liniers' character and capability as a leader had come into question and his image in the eyes of the people was seriously affected.

Also, from this time onwards there was continual discord between the Commandant of Arms and the Cabildo. It was the duty of the former to report back to the king of Spain, but his report of the recapture of Buenos Aires mentioned nothing of the bravery of the people, preferring instead to give the credit to the handful of regular troops Liniers had brought with him from Montevideo. This caused an outrage amongst the people and their representative voice, the Cabildo, and although Liniers sent a second report to Spain to repair the injustice the damage was done and an unfortunate rivalry developed between the two. A consequence of this affair was that Juan Martin Pueyrredon, one of the heroes of the *reconquista*, as it had become known, was sent to Spain with orders to explain to the king just exactly what had happened.

Meanwhile, preparations were made to transport the British prisoners inland, and on 2 September the rank and file, under their sergeants, began their journey inland in wagons. They were split up into six groups, 400 being sent to Cordoba, 200 each to Mendoza and San Juan, 100 each to Santiago del Estero and San Luis, and a further 200 to Tucuman, whilst the wounded remained in Buenos Aires. The governor of Santiago del Estero reported that the 71st Regiment had arrived there almost naked as a consequence of their uniforms being taken from them to dress a regiment of *Migueletes*, or Spanish light horse. The men were to stay in the provinces for the next ten months and inevitably came into contact with the local people. At Cordoba, where the largest group was sent, they would not obey their guards and, having caused much trouble, had to be split up again, some being moved to Alte Gracia and some to Carlota. The women who had followed their husbands to the Rio de la Plata also went into captivity and later on, when they were released, many stayed on to settle in the colony amongst their newly found friends.

The British officers remained in Buenos Aires until 11 October. They were well treated by the people and a farewell lunch was organised when they were moved inland. They reached Lujan on the 12th and Beresford, Pack and seven other officers were billeted in the mansion house. The rest arrived at Capilla on the 14th and other at San Antonio de Areco on the 16th. Here they were to stay for the next three months playing cricket, shooting and generally having a pleasant time of it. Sir Home Popham, still moored in the river, re-embarked the few remaining detachments of free British troops still ashore and then withdrew his ships and sailed down river to a safer anchorage to await British reinforcements from Cape Colony.

The reconquest of Buenos Aires was complete but the inhabitants of the colony felt sure that Britain would not give up so easily and that it would only be a matter of time before another army appeared on the scene to threaten them. On 6 September, therefore, the Commandant of Arms published a proclamation in agreement with that determined upon on 14 August by the Cabildo, calling upon the people to arm themselves in view of the possible new threat posed by the presence of the British still moored in the river. The order was given and they formed themselves into five regiments according to their province of origin in Spain. In this way the beginning of Liniers' 'new army' was formed. The 'European' Spaniards, that is to say Spanish people residing in Buenos Aires, were thus formed into five regiments: the Cuerpo de Gallegos, and the Tercios de Andaluces, Catalanes, Vizcainos and Montanese. Liniers felt, however, that he needed more than these five regiments to repulse any other possible attacks but a Royal Order, dated 28 February 1795, stipulated that the viceroy could only impose emergency measures for defence in conjunction with a *junta de guerra*, or war council, consisting of the Intendant and senior officers of the garrison. Therefore, Liniers did just that and formed a *junta* in order to create the volunteer corps that would form the 'New Army'.

There were five squadrons of militia cavalry in Buenos Aires and these formed the basis for the six new regiments that were created: the 1st Husares de Pueyrredon, the Husares Cazadores o Infernales, the Escuadron de Carabineros de Carlos IV, the Escuadron de Migueletes de Caballeria, the Cuerpo de Quinteros o Labradores and the Escuadron auxiliar de Caballeria de la Maestranza de Artilleria. These then were the cavalry. The inhabitants of the colony then formed themselves into infantry and artillery units: The Cuerpo de Patricios, formed from the natives of Buenos Aires, and still in existence today, the Cuerpo Arribenos, the Batallon de Naturales, Pardos y Morenos de Infanteria, the Compania de Granaderos de Infanteria, the Batallon de Marina, the Cuerpo de Patriotas de la Union, the Cuerpo de Artilleria de Indios, Pardos y Morenos and the Cuerpo de Esclaves.

Liniers' call for volunteers went unanswered by large sections of the population and a decree of conscription was issued on 20 November 1806, making all men between the ages of 16 and 50 liable for service, except for the clergy, officials, slaves and the physically handicapped. He also forbade people to leave the city. Enlistment was still not total, however, so finally on 5 February 1807, he issued a second decree ordering the impressment of all men who had still not enlisted. Colonel Pedro Arce was appointed Sub-Inspector of these forces, but he had little authority as battalion commanders appointed their own officers at will and organised their units as they saw fit. He protested to Sobremonte who could do nothing. Sobremonte himself was most unhappy at the creation of the volunteer units as he saw them as a threat to Spanish rule in the colony. On 30 December 1806, he wrote a letter to Manuel Godoy, in Spain, in which he said:

> ...the system of defence which has been adopted out of necessity is not favourable: people armed en masse are very exposed to subversion and their training in the use of arms offers few advantages in actions where all wish to command and few to obey.[16]

Sobremonte was also disturbed by the thought of the people keeping arms in their own homes in case they used them for the wrong purposes. But whatever doubts Sobremonte may have had about Liniers' new army it was not long before it was put to the test.

IV

The Fall of Montevideo

On 13 September 1806, one month after his surrender, Beresford's original report of his capture of Buenos Aires arrived in London along with Popham's circular. When the news broke London's commercial world went wild with delight. Businessmen were gripped by visions of new markets and they saw huge profits to be made, none of them stopping to even think about or consider the great distances involved and despite the fact that British merchants had already been for a long time exporting goods to South America in neutral ships. The best they could probably hope for was a cheaper tariff but this did not seem to matter to them and the city buzzed in anticipation of its expected fortunes.

The rejoicing reached new heights when the treasure captured by Beresford arrived from the Rio de la Plata. It was landed from the *Narcissus* at Portsmouth, from where it was taken in triumph to London. On Saturday, 20 September, at eleven o'clock in the morning, the Loyal Britons Volunteers mustered in St. James's Square to escort the captured treasure to London. On their arrival at Clapham they found waiting for them a cavalcade consisting of eight wagons, each drawn by six horses, adorned with flags, pennants and blue ribbons. On the flags was inscribed the word 'treasure' and each of the wagons was preceded by a brass field piece taken from the enemy. The first wagon bore the viceroyalty standard of Peru which was displayed by a royal marine, the second and third the colours taken from the walls of Buenos Aires whilst those following bore the English blue, red and white naval ensigns, the whole making a grand and triumphal spectacle. A band belonging to the Clapham Volunteers played 'God Save the King', 'Rule Britannia', etc, and as it was reported in the newspapers at the time, 'every Briton's heart rejoiced at the scene.'

Having entered London they stopped at the Admiralty then proceeded up Pall Mall to St. James's Square where the procession halted. It was then presented with a pair of colours on which was written in gold letters on blue silk within laurel branches the words, 'Buenos Aires, Popham, Beresford, Victory.' The treasure then passed through the city to the Bank where upwards of two million dollars were deposited. On the front of each wagon appeared the words, 'treasure chest,' and it was noted that, 'The windows were uncommonly crowded with spectators anxious to witness the triumph of Old England. Captain Donnelly, of the *Narcissus*, rode in a poste-chaise in the procession.'

The British government, however, was too concerned with events in Europe and did not totally share the people's jubilation. But such was the clamour for action to be taken in support of Beresford's small British force that the government was eventually obliged to act. It will be remembered that Baird had already despatched a reinforcement of just over two thousand men from the Cape of Good Hope, under Lieutenant-Colonel Backhouse. Now, on receiving Beresford's despatch, another force was ordered to the Rio de la Plata.

This force had been scheduled to sail earlier in support of Beresford but had become earmarked for Portugal instead. On the abandonment of that particular project, however, it was again ordered to South America. It consisted of just under three thousand men and was commanded by Sir Samuel Auchmuty.

Fifty-one years old, Auchmuty had a distinguished career behind him and had gained his rank by merit alone. Born in New York he joined the 45th Regiment to fight against the rebels during the War of Independence and saw action at Brooklyn and White Plains. He was rewarded for his loyalty with an ensigncy in 1777 and the following year a lieutenancy without purchase. At the end of the war he returned to England but found he could not afford to live on his lieutenant's pay and so in 1783 he exchanged into the 52nd Regiment, bound for India. He saw service there against Hyder Ali and in 1788 was promoted captain. He served in the campaigns of 1790 and 1791 against Tippoo Sultan and was present at Seringapatam in 1792. When he returned to England in 1795 he did so as a lieutenant-colonel after having left England's shores fourteen years earlier with the rank of lieutenant. In 1800 he was ordered to the Red Sea to co-operate with Sir David Baird in assisting Abercromby in Egypt against the French. Like Baird and Beresford, Auchmuty was to become one of the heroes of the march across the desert. In 1803, he was made a knight of the Bath and three years later was made colonel of the 103rd Regiment.

Auchmuty's orders simply stated that on arrival in South America he was to place himself under Beresford's command, and in case the latter should find himself in any difficulty or to have surrendered he was to secure a footing and await further reinforcements. If the situation looked totally hopeless he was to return to the Cape of Good Hope. On 9 October, Auchmuty's force sailed for the Rio de la Plata.

Four days after Auchmuty's departure the reinforcements sent by Baird from the Cape, under Backhouse, arrived and entered the Rio de la Plata to learn to their total astonishment that the Spaniards had recaptured Buenos Aires and that Beresford and his men were being held prisoners. This placed Backhouse in a difficult and unenviable position. He had under him just over two thousand troops, was in an alien country and had no orders. He was totally isolated and had no way of knowing what course of action his government might want him to take.

Popham was still moored in the river, however, and after some discussion it was decided at first to attempt the capture of Montevideo owing to its important strategic position as a strong and secure base from which to act. The plan was later abandoned because the water was too shallow to allow the ships to come in close enough to bombard the town, and in any case there was probably an insufficient number of troops to carry out the operation. Eventually Backhouse decided to make a landing on the coast of Banda Oriental, what is now Uruguay, which he did on 29 October.

Disembarking with four hundred men of the 38th Regiment under Colonel Vassal Backhouse immediately advanced against the small town of Maldonado which was occupied by about six hundred regular Spanish troops and militia with two pieces of artillery. Backhouse's despatch read:

> To the cool intrepidity of our little column, on this occasion, much praise is due, as it advanced with the utmost steadiness and alacrity, and without firing a shot, until sufficiently near to make a certainty of carrying both the guns and the town, which was principally done by the bayonet, notwithstanding the advance was made under heavy discharges of grape and musketry.[1]

The Spaniards were swept away at a cost to the 38th Regiment of two killed and four wounded, the defenders losing about fifty men. The following day, with the help of the marines and seamen from Popham's ships, Backhouse forced the surrender of the island of Goretti with its 32-gun batteries, as well as an arsenal containing a great number of swords, muskets and pistols. For the next few days Backhouse was able to obtain horses for his cavalry and as the enemy kept well back he was able to secure supplies without too much trouble. It was not long, however, before a build up of enemy troops began around Maldonado and things began to worsen for the British.

The situation deteriorated daily for them as supplies dwindled and it became difficult for them to find any around the vicinity of the town. After taking away from the surrounding area all which might be of use to the British the local commandant, Moreno, kept a constant watch in order to prevent the small detachments which were being sent out from

Maldonado from securing supplies, horses and forage. Facing this situation Backhouse decided to send out larger units capable of overcoming enemy resistance and able to go farther in order to get what was needed. One such group consisted one hundred and twenty infantry and sixty dragoons and on 7 November started out for the village of San Carlos, about eight miles away.

Meanwhile, a retired naval lieutenant, Agustin Abreu, had just received orders from the Marquis de Sobremonte, now in Montevideo, to select a small force and march for Maldonado where he was to harass the British and prevent them from procuring supplies, and also to stop them advancing inland. Abreu duly left for Maldonado at the head of ninety dragoons, as many Cordobeses and one hundred and fifty of the Regimiento de Voluntario Caballeria de Montevideo. On his arrival in the area, on the 7th, he was told that a British party was heading for San Carlos and he immediately decided to march and face them. Whilst the British were at San Carlos, they likewise learned that Abreu's force was advancing on them and without wasting any time prepared to receive the attack.

The British took up a position on a plain to the west of the village, the dragoons drawn up in two lines with the infantry to their right in a square. To the south of the plain lay a hill which Abreu's detachment had to climb. On reaching the top they spread out across the plain and formed a long arc with their lines overlapping the British flanks. Having given the order to attack, Abreu led the right flank with his dragoons who made a charge against the British cavalry, whilst the Cordobese and the Regimiento de Montevideo followed. When the two Spanish detachments came into range of the British infantry the latter opened up, badly mauling them and forcing them to the right following the dragoons. Here, the British cavalry had got into some difficulty and their infantry had to come to their assistance. The movement of the British infantry exposed the left flank of the Spanish column to attack and after some hand to hand fighting the column was forced to retreat. At this moment Abreu was mortally wounded, as was his second-in-command, Captain Jose Martinez, and on seeing this the Spaniards fell into complete disarray and disorder and were soon in headlong retreat, it being impossible to regroup them with the victorious British snapping at their heels.

The pursuit did not continue very far and as soon as they had reorganised themselves the British, who had suffered casualties of about ten killed and wounded, marched back to Maldonado. The Spanish casualties were slightly higher. Agustin Abreu died of his wounds four days later, as did Captain Martinez. Another officer, Francisco Huiz, of the Montevideo Volunteers, was also wounded. After the action the Spanish troops regrouped and led by Commandant Moreno they settled down around Maldonado to keep the British penned in. The British themselves did not attempt any similar expeditions and by daily skirmishing were gradually forced back within the town where, totally cut off and isolated, they had no choice but to wait and hope that they could hold out until the arrival of British reinforcements.

Back in London, meanwhile, events were about to take an amazing and almost unbelievable turn. During the month of October 1806, the Secretary of State, William Windham, evolved 'one of the most astonishing plans that ever emanated from the brain even of a British Minister of War.'[2]

Up until now the British government had been reluctant to pay too much attention to affairs in South America but with public opinion clamouring for action following Beresford's capture of Buenos Aires it did an amazing turnabout. Based purely on the assumption that the British army's reputation and superiority would precede it, Windham proposed to send a larger force to consolidate British gains in South America. The officer chosen to command the expedition was his friend, Brigadier-General Robert Craufurd, 'Black Bob', who was to gain almost legendary status commanding the Light Division to glory under Wellington in the Peninsular War.

Craufurd was born in 1764 and at the age of sixteen was gazetted as an ensign in the 65th Regiment, transferring to the 26th Regiment the same year. In 1782, after reaching the rank of captain, he went on half-pay and the year after went abroad to study military art. He returned to England in 1787 a very educated officer, something of a rarity then. But opportunities in the army were few and Craufurd became bitter at seeing many uneducated officers being promoted around him. However, he obtained command of the 75th Regiment when it was raised in 1787 and went with it to India where he served with distinction under Lord Cornwallis. Disenchanted, however, he resigned from the army in 1794 and travelled to Italy and Germany to accompany his brother, Lieutenant-Colonel Charles Craufurd, who had been appointed a Special Commissioner with the Archduke Charles of Austria. Craufurd saw much action during the next three years as an observer although it has also been suggested that he may have been employed as a secret agent by the Foreign Office.

Upon his return to England he began to press his claims for employment once again with the British army. He was by now an officer of great ability, was well versed in every branch of military art and was not one to hide his light under a bushel. In 1798 he was appointed Deputy-Quartermaster General to the Forces in Ireland under his old chief, Lord Cornwallis, and throughout that year led a flying column against the Irish rebels. After the rebellion was crushed he again left for Switzerland as part of a military mission to Austria but was recalled shortly after and was appointed to the staff of the Duke of York in Holland during the expedition of 1799. By 1802 he was a lieutenant-colonel but in July that year he resigned from the army when he was elected as M.P. for East Retford. He sat in the House of Commons for the next four years and gained the title of 'the Colonel' and spoke regularly on military matters. He was a great friend of William Windham who obtained various appointments for him and it was he who got him promoted to Colonel in October 1805.

On hearing of Beresford's successful expedition in 1806 Craufurd wrote to Windham asking for command of the forces in South America, the upshot being that he was indeed appointed, but this lasted only until he was superseded by Whitelocke in 1807. The real glory for Craufurd, however, was to come later under Wellington in the Peninsula. Craufurd received two letters from Windham, both dated 30 October, in which he set out his ambitious plan. The main aim of the expedition was to secure a strong footing on the west coast of Chile from where Craufurd would set about the reduction of the rest of that country. He was to pledge Britain's protection for that country and was to go to great lengths to show the people that this, and not the quest for wealth and treasure, was the purpose of his mission. He was not to incite or encourage any revolts in the neighbouring provinces and was to ensure that peace, law and order were maintained. As soon as Chile was in British hands Craufurd was to make contact with Beresford and somehow establish a chain of military posts between himself and Buenos Aires. This was the plan but in view of Popham's pirate-like raid on Buenos Aires it is difficult to imagine the Chilean people accepting Craufurd's claims that protection was the pretext of his mission and not booty, and how he was to establish the chain of posts across the Andes through nearly a thousand miles of enemy infested country Windham did not explain. As the historian of the British Army later wrote:

> Military officers by incapacity and misjudgement have often placed Ministers in situations of cruel difficulty, but it may be doubted whether any General has ever set them a task quite so impossible as that prescribed, not in the doubt and turmoil of a campaign but in the tranquillity of the closet, by Windham to Craufurd.[3]

These wild ideas from the Ministry did not stop here, however. Lord Grenville came up with a similarly fantastic idea for an attack upon, of all places, Mexico. This ingenious plan involved an attack from the east by six thousand European troops and from the west by a further thousand European troops, with four thousand sepoys from India who were to attack Manila and capture the Philippines on the way! Grenville soon realised, however, that it would be almost impossible to co-ordinate both attacks at the same time but he still thought his plan possible and was prepared to modify his plan and attack from the west only rather than see the whole plan abandoned altogether. Therefore, in November, Grenville requested none other than Sir Arthur Wellesley to draw up a feasibility study of his plan and also upon a proposed attack upon Venezuela. It was all quite incredible.

Fortunately, the voice of sanity must have been heard because the fantastic plan was abandoned although Windham still thought his own plan to take Chile to be possible and Craufurd continued his preparations in the utmost secrecy. As the troops began to assemble for the expedition they naturally wondered where they were going and there was much speculation and curiosity as to their destination, so much so, in fact, that it became known as the 'secret' or 'remote' expedition. Craufurd's force consisted of 4,300 men. Some of these had been embarked some weeks beforehand and were eventually to spend nearly nine months aboard ship, although their officers saw to it that every man remained as healthy as possible. In addition to Craufurd's own men, eight troops of the 9th Light Dragoons were to join the expedition and depart along the way for the Rio de la Plata to join Auchmuty's reinforcements leaving Craufurd to sail on to Chile. These were originally part of Auchmuty's force but problems with their transport ships made it necessary for them to return to port until another naval escort could be found for them. The convoy consisted of forty transports and merchantmen and was to be escorted by four ships of the line and numerous other vessels. The naval squadron was under the command of Commodore Stopford who, at the Cape de Verde islands, was to be replaced by Admiral Murray who would become naval commander-in-chief of the expedition.

On 12 November 1806, after much delay, the convoy sailed from Falmouth bound for the west coast of South America. The expedition reached the Cape de Verde islands on 14 December, anchoring in Porto Praya. Murray had not yet arrived so there was nothing to do but to wait for him. An uneventful three weeks passed, the 9th Light Dragoons were sent off to the Rio de la Plata according to orders with the frigate *Nercide* as escort, but still there was no sign of Murray. Craufurd soon grew tired of waiting and decided he could do so no longer. He persuaded Commodore Stopford to escort him as far as the Cape of Good Hope and on 11 January 1807, the convoy set off once again. As it happened, Admiral Murray reached Porto Praya shortly after Craufurd's departure and set off immediately for the Cape which, ironically, he was to reach before Craufurd. Here, the story takes another turn.

Twenty days after Craufurd's departure from Falmouth the *Diadem* arrived in England bringing the news from Buenos Aires that the city had been recaptured by the Spaniards and that Beresford and his men were being held prisoner. A drastic rethink was needed and consequently, the British government despatched the fastest brig in the navy, the *Fly*, to catch up with Murray at the Cape with orders for himself and Craufurd to proceed straight to the Rio de la Plata where they were to assist Auchmuty with the recapture of Buenos Aires.

Auchmuty himself had also been sent new orders instructing him to take the city, and when successful was to send Craufurd on to carry out his original mission to Chile. On 23 March, Craufurd reached the Cape where he found Murray awaiting him with the new orders and on 6 April they set out across the Atlantic for their new destination, reaching St. Helena on the 21st and sailing again five days later for the Rio de la Plata. Here we must leave Craufurd's expedition to return to the progress made by the British reinforcements under Sir Samuel Auchmuty.

Auchmuty's force had undergone a tiring journey since leaving England in October. On 14 December they had reached Rio de Janeiro where the convoy put in to take on water and provisions. Some of the troops went ashore for exercise and whilst there, were reviewed by the Queen of Portugal who presented them with pumpkins and onions! It was also whilst at Rio that Auchmuty received the news of the reconquest by the Spaniards of Buenos Aires, and that a British force of unknown strength had occupied Maldonado. He remained at Rio for a week before resuming his journey to the Rio de la Plata and on 5 January the convoy crawled slowly into the river and moored off Maldonado.

Auchmuty found Backhouse's men in a poor state, surrounded and constantly harassed by enemy cavalry who were skilled riders, able to ride up, dismount and fire over the backs of their horses before riding off again at great speed. Backhouse's supplies had dwindled away and it was virtually impossible for him to obtain fresh provisions with these horsemen always hovering around the town.

> We found the remains of the army in the greatest want of everything necessary belonging to an army and quite disheartened. On the land side they were surrounded by about 400 horsemen who cut off all their foraging parties and intercepted all supplies. These horsemen were not regular soldiers, but the inhabitants of the country who had turned out to defend their homes from the enemy. [4]

It was obvious to Auchmuty that to remain at Maldonado would serve no useful purpose and he decided to evacuate the place whilst leaving a small detachment to garrison the island of Goretti. It was also obvious that the combined forces of both Auchmuty and Backhouse, though numbering around 5000, were still too weak to attempt an attack on Buenos Aires. Therefore, after conferring with Admiral Sterling, who had replaced Popham, Auchmuty decided that the only sensible choice open to him was to take the town of Montevideo. The tactical reasons behind making an attempt on this place, good fortifications giving a secure base from which to operate, have already been stated earlier. The town would also give him strong protection against enemy forces until the arrival of Craufurd's men. Only then would they have sufficient strength to make a second attempt on Buenos Aires. Accordingly, on 13 January, the British troops pulled out of Maldonado, leaving behind the small garrison on Goretti, and sailed further up the coast to a small bay just west of the Caretas rocks, nine miles below Montevideo.

On the morning of the 16th, Auchmuty's men began to disembark at a place called Buceo. A large contingent of Spanish troops with guns were in a position a short distance from the landing place but they made no real attempt to dispute the landing:

> ...boats were ordered alongside the troopships to convey us on shore, which movement, as the enemy was on the banks about fifteen thousand strong to oppose us, put a rather nasty taste into our mouths, there seeming nothing but death or glory before us. The signal was hoisted from the admiral's ship, and we started for the shore amid the fire of the enemy's artillery. They killed and wounded a few of our men, and sank some of the boats, but as soon as we struck the shore, we jumped out, and forming line in the water, fired a volley and charged, soon driving them from their position on the bank. We found even as early as then that Spaniards were not very difficult to encounter. In case of a retreat, our boats were still within our reach, but having gained the victory we had no need of them, stopping where we were on the banks all night.[5]

The British troops pushed forward quickly and took up positions about a mile inland in order to cover the landing of the stores and supplies. A detachment of the 95th Rifles covered the advance and in the skirmish with some local Spanish troops lost a bugler killed and Lieutenant Chawner wounded. The first troops to land were the 95th, 38th and the Light Battalion, along with Brigadier-General Lumley, Lieutenant-Colonel Bourke, Major Tucker and Brigade-Major Roach. They pushed inland under cover of a well directed fire from H.M.S. *Charwell* and the gun-brig *Encounter*. Auchmuty himself landed afterwards to take command, pushing his men forward to occupy some heights in front of them. The rest of the army landed under the watchful eye of Colonel Browne, of the 40th, to consolidate the position whilst the landings continued.

> Some field pieces were next on shore, and likewise a number of sailors with drag ropes to work them, as we had no horses with us, and up to this time no artillery. The country was rather favourable to the sailors, being very level and mostly green pasture, so that they kept along pretty easily, seeming just in their glory, all this being new work to them.[6]

The British army remained upon the heights throughout the 17th and 18th whilst the field train and the last of the supplies were landed. There was frequent skirmishing between the Spanish troops and the advanced

British piquets, mainly riflemen, and during these two days the navy gave vital assistance with the *Encounter* and an armed transport giving protection to Auchmuty's left flank by keeping up a steady fire on the Spanish troops that appeared there, dislodging them from their positions. At daybreak on 19 January the army formed into three columns, the right under Lumley, the left under Browne and the reserve under Backhouse and soon the whole army was on the move towards Montevideo.

Montevideo, the principal port of the colony of the Rio de la Plata, was a much more strongly fortified town than Buenos Aires and would be a tougher nut to crack. The town was situated on the northern shore of the Rio de la Plata and took its name from the mountain situated on the opposite side of the harbour. It was built on a rocky slope jutting out from the mainland and was surrounded on three sides by the sea. The fortifications stretched right round the town with the sea defences consisting of thirteen heavily built batteries which were connected by a curtain or covered way. The approach to these was difficult owing to the rocky nature of the shore. The batteries were also protected by a fort called the St. Philip, which was situated at the north-west angle of the peninsula. The landward side formed a salient with the southern face being a thousand yards long and the northern face twelve hundred. The walls were four feet thick and fifteen feet high and at the point of the salient angle there was constructed a strong fort called the Citadel. This was covered by a ravelin and by ditches and the only entrance into it was from within the town itself across a small drawbridge, the entrance being protected by twenty guns and four mortars.

The Citadel was flanked on either side by 9-gun batteries mounted on demi-bastions and beyond these stood two more demi-bastions with fourteen guns on the north side and seven on the south. There were two entrances to the town known as the North and South Gates, the North being situated between the Citadel and the fourteen gun battery and the South a hundred yards from the river. The South Gate was also protected not only by the seven-gun battery but also by two heavy guns mounted on a round tower near the water. Altogether, Montevideo was protected by one hundred and thirteen pieces of artillery with twenty-four of them in the Citadel and forty more on the landward side. Near the Citadel was the cathedral, a large brick building with two lofty towers, which was situated on the western face of an open square. The streets were similar to those in Buenos Aires in that they were laid out at right angles to each other and the houses were likewise made of brick and had flat roofs. The ground outside the walls of the town was rough and uneven and broken by gullies. This area was occupied by several small houses, most of which had been destroyed at the approach of the British army.

The governor of the town, Ruiz Huidobro, had done his best to get the town's defences into a sufficient state to resist the coming attack but with such minimal resources at hand was obviously at a disadvantage. He knew, however, that he could depend on the people for support and the garrison of the town was preparing itself to meet the British invaders. As well as these there was always the chance that help might be forthcoming from Buenos Aires but communication was difficult between the two owing to the presence of the Royal Navy moored in the bay off the town. Huidobro placed Bernado Suarez in command of the defences, and he quickly set to work organising the local militia. There was also the Marquis de Sobremonte, still attempting to display his authority, who had brought with him to Montevideo a cavalry force from Cordoba and Santa Fe, with Colonel Allende as his second-in-command. In all, the Spanish force defending the town was a mixture of all kinds of militia, regular troops and local people, with little discipline but plenty of bravery and led by officers with very little experience of warfare.

The British army continued its march, negotiating heavy sand dunes with the seamen struggling to keep the guns rolling and late on 19 January the two opposing armies came into view. Sobremonte had brought a large part of the garrison with him, nearly 2,500 men in all, and took up a position on some heights to the left and right of them. He formed his men into two lines with the first consisting of about 1,700 of his cavalry with two 8-pounders and two mortars under Colonel Allende. The second line consisted of 260 men of the Regimiento de Infanteria de Buenos Aires and 340 of the Cuerpo de Husares Voluntarios. These were joined by 200 militia with nine guns.

The Spanish troops opened up a heavy fire of grape and round shot upon the British as Allende's column advanced, supported by infantry. His cavalry bore down hard on the British infantry but they were met by a counter-attack by the Light Battalion under Brownrigg. At this point another British attack threatened the Spaniards' line of retreat and caused a great deal of confusion in their ranks. One of the first to flee from the action was, of course, the Marquis de Sobremonte, who fled from the field followed by his cavalry in the greatest disorder. A general retreat soon began and the remaining troops were left to fight on hopelessly outnumbered, although the regular troops of the Regimiento de Buenos Aires and the Cuerpo de Husares made an orderly withdrawal, fighting as they went. The rest of the Spanish troops, mainly militia, had already fallen back to Montevideo, retreating as soon as the order was given by Huidobro who was totally dismayed by Sobremonte's inept performance as military commander.

The action cost Auchmuty twenty-five killed and wounded but the Spaniards suffered considerably higher casualties in this short action which now left the way to Montevideo wide open, and although a cannonading continued from the ramparts of the town there were now no enemy troops outside it and Auchmuty was able to advance unopposed to the suburbs which had by now been evacuated.

As the march on Montevideo continued the British troops were joined by about eight hundred sailors, Royal Marines and pikemen, under the orders of Captain Donnelly, whom Admiral Sterling had landed. Sterling had also ordered boats to go in close by the shore to keep a look out for any wounded men and bring them off, whilst covering vessels were positioned in order to prevent any attacks the enemy might make.

On the morning of 20 January another attempt was made to stop the advance when part of the garrison of Montevideo marched out to make a sortie. They were under the command of Bernado Lecocq, of the engineers, and he had with him 2,362 men as well as Sobremonte's 1,700 cavalry who still hovered on the scene. They also had a few guns with them. The two forces met at a place called El Cristo and almost immediately the Spanish infantry was engaged by piquets of the 87th Regiment, numbering about 400, under Major Miller. The 87th stood firm but were soon in danger of being overrun by the sheer weight of enemy numbers until Colonel Browne, in command of the British left, ordered forward three companies of the 40th Regiment. These troops formed up and charged the Spanish column and a bitter hand-to-hand struggle ensued with numbers falling on both sides.

The Spaniards held firm until Auchmuty ordered forward the 95th Rifles and the Light Battalion who attacked the flank of the column. The British gave three cheers and set about the enemy with a furious charge which sent the Spaniards reeling before they gave way completely. The mounted column, which had so far taken no part in the action, also retreated, with the Husares under Captain Mordeil again distinguishing themselves whilst attempting to cover the retreat of the infantry who were being vigorously pursued by the victorious British infantry.

Sobremonte's cavalry again behaved badly, retreating without even attempting to engage the British and then abandoning the field altogether, leaving their comrades to fight on alone. It was said that they did not stop riding until they were thirty miles away. Not all of the Spanish troops showed this lack of courage, however. We have already seen the cavalry under the Frenchman, Mordeil, distinguishing himself at the head of the Husares, and now another officer, Martin Guemes, a lieutenant in the regular army, showed great courage in resisting the advancing British troops. His company stood firm and made a gallant stand inspiring other units to stop and join them, holding out for some time before the British finally forced them to abandon their position and retreat. Guemes was later to become a hero as a gaucho leader who led his men in the wars of independence in Argentina.

The action at El Cristo cost the garrison between two and three hundred killed with as many wounded. Auchmuty's losses were seventy-two killed and wounded. Once again there was criticism of the display given by Sobremonte's cavalry. In a letter to the Cabildo in Buenos Aires dated

23 January, Pereyra, of the Regimiento de Buenos Aires, described the action:

> ...on the 20th of this month a force composed of 4000, including 1000 horsemen that had been gathered from the former regiment of the Viceroy (who is absent), each small corps being equipped with two guns opened a battle at seven in the morning that lasted for at least an hour and a half with incessant firing, until our army fell into an ambush. So far, we are ignorant of the number of dead: three hundred of our men were captured, there are two hundred wounded and of the Viceroy's troops not one single man was to be found in the place.[7]

The British victory had at least one significant effect. Namely, that instead of continuing a constant harassment of the British outposts and piquets, the Spanish horsemen kept well away within the walls of Montevideo itself and the British were allowed to settle down to the business of laying siege to the place. As two British soldiers themselves put it:

> After this action, we saw no more of our troublesome guests, the horsemen, who used to brave us in our lines and even wound our people in the camp.[8]

> We never found the Spaniards sally out of the town after this to engage us, as I expect they did not much like the hot reception they had received.[9]

For the British, the action at El Cristo was the most costly of their campaign in the Rio de la Plata so far. Indeed, the seventy-two casualties suffered by Auchmuty in this one action alone was some seven times the casualties suffered by Beresford when he captured Buenos Aires the year before, and with the many Spanish dead and wounded the battlefield that evening was a grim sight:

> As the battalion to which I belonged returned from the pursuit, we passed in our way to the camp, over the field of the dead. It was too much for my feelings; I was obliged to turn aside my head from the horrid sight. The birds of prey seemed to contend with those who were burying the slain for the possession of the bodies. Horrid sight! Men who in the morning, exulted, trod forth in strength; whose minds, only fettered by their bodies, seemed to feel restraint, now lay shockingly mangled and a prey to animals.[10]

Even experienced soldiers, like William Lawrence, in a strange land, felt an unusual uneasiness:

I remember that I happened to be placed that night on sentry at the road leading to the town, and not far from a hole where we had buried five or six hundred of the enemy. It was the most uncomfortable two hours' sentry I have ever spent as yet, and I kept my eyes more on the place where the dead were than on the road I was placed to watch, not having altogether forgotten the absurd ghost stories of my own country.[11]

Now that the Spaniards had been driven back into Montevideo Auchmuty could turn his attention to the capture of the place without any interference from the enemy. The Spanish troops, however, still held the island of Ratones which commanded the harbour with its formidable batteries. It was obvious that these guns were capable of creating havoc amongst the British troops constructing the siege batteries which would be used to breach the walls of the town, and it was here that the navy gave great assistance.

The frigates, gun-brigs and armed transports, commanded by Captain Honeyman, of H.M.S. *Leda*, kept up a steady fire upon the batteries in the harbour and diverted the attention of the Spanish gunners. By doing so, it allowed the British troops some measure of relief from the guns. Auchmuty landed several 24-pounders from the men-of-war, and a battery of six guns and a second of four guns and one mortar were established to fire against the walls of the Citadel. These opened fire on 21 January and a great number of shots found their targets against the south-east bastion which, although they did great damage, did not breach the wall. On the 23rd another battery, consisting of just two guns, was constructed and opened fire on the enemy gunboats which still slipped into the harbour bringing supplies, stores and water to the besieged garrison. On 25 January the batteries of four 24-pounders and two mortars opened fire and all the frigates and smaller vessels came in as close as they could to bombard the town.

Whilst the British troops worked at constructing the siege batteries they came under a constant, if not heavy, fire from the town with round-shot, grape and shells that flew in amongst them:

The bursting of shells, or lodging of balls, within a few yards of the light battalion, was constantly a subject of merriment and witticisms; such was the spirited coolness they attained from the example of their intrepid commanders.[12]

The British found the walls much stronger than had been anticipated and to add to Auchmuty's problems there was a shortage of entrenching tools and even more seriously an ever dwindling supply of gunpowder. But still the men worked on:

We set to work building up batteries and breastworks some three hundred of us being sent to cut down a copse of peach trees that was near to make gabions and fascines to form them with. When our fortifications were completed, which was in a very few days, we began bombarding the town, for which purpose we had brought up our twenty-four pounders from the men-of-war.[13]

For new recruits the work was new and the fatigue great:

Constructing batteries and other works, we were forced to labour night and day. My hands, when I left home, were white and soft; now they were excoriated and brown and, where they were unbroken, as hard as horn. Often overpowered by fatigue, sleep has sealed my eyes; I have awoke groaning with thirst, and the intense heat of my hands.[14]

On 28 January a battery of six 24-pounders was constructed a thousand yards from the Citadel and soon the shots began to pound against it. Before long the guns had reduced the parapet to ruins but still no breach was made in the walls. The powder supply grew shorter and in a last attempt at breaching the walls another battery of six guns was constructed six hundred yards from the wall by the South Gate. The Spanish garrison opened up a heavy fire on this battery but with little effect and on 2 February it was reported to Auchmuty that a practicable breach had been made in the wall. This was timely news for the British commander for it had become known to him that a Spanish force was on its way to attempt the relief of the town.

There were, in fact, two relief forces on their way to Montevideo. The first was under the command of Sub-Inspector Pedro Arce, and consisted of 511 men who had disembarked at San Juan, just north of Colonia, on 26 January, marching to Rosario and then Las Piedras. Here, Arce received orders from Sobremonte to the effect that he was to go no further as the town was sure to fall and that the loss of an extra five hundred men would serve the Spaniards' cause no good at all. Arce, however, disobeyed this order and continued on, slipping past the British vessels in the harbour and entering the town on the night of 2 February.

A second relief expedition was also planned with a larger force, to be led by Liniers himself. The Spaniards' leader met with fierce opposition from the Cabildo which forbade him to go, probably because they feared it would weaken their own defences in Buenos Aires. However, on 29 January the expedition, consisting of 1,350 men with six guns, sailed from Banda Oriental. Liniers reached Conchillas the following day and dispatched an officer to Montevideo to inform Huidobro that he must try and hold out for at least another four days, the earliest time by which help could be got to him. But it was not to be, for even as Liniers' force hurried on towards the besieged town news arrived informing him of its fall and Liniers was left with no choice but to return to Buenos Aires, which he reached on 8 February.

Auchmuty, meanwhile, was aware of these approaching relief forces and dare not delay the assault any longer, even though it meant exposing his men to a heavy fire on entering the breach. Given time he may have been able to starve the garrison into submission and so avoid any casualties at all but with Spanish troops closing in all the time he was left with no choice but to make an assault. On the evening of 2 February a summons was sent to Huidobro to surrender the town. No answer was returned, however, and so the assault was on.

The attack was to take place on the morning of the 3rd and the troops destined to make the assault were the 95th, under Major Gardiner, the Light Battalion, under Brownrigg and Major Trotter, and the 38th Regiment under Vassal and Nugent. These were to be supported by the 40th and the 87th. The storming parties were under the command of Browne. The 'Forlorn Hope' consisted mainly of men from the 54th, under Lieutenant Everard and a sergeant of the 38th. The 87th Regiment and one company of the 95th were sent to the North Gate which was to be opened to them once the stormers were inside.

At three o'clock on the morning of 3 February, in extreme darkness, the storming parties stole forward and moved silently towards the breach. They entered the ditch but in the darkness could not find the breach which, in fact, the garrison had hidden by covering it with bullocks' hides filled with earth. As the 95th looked in vain for the opening the alarm was raised and a storm of grape shot and musketry was opened up on them from the walls, the exposed column reeling back with men dropping on every side. For fifteen minutes or so the British troops struggled in the dark at the foot of the walls and here Colonel Brownrigg, leading the Light Battalion, was fatally wounded.

At last, however, Captain Renny, of the 40th, found the breach and led his men to it. It was only wide enough to allow in three men abreast at one time and from the top of it to the town beyond there was a drop of twelve feet. Renny led his men to the top of the breach but was tragically shot dead as he reached it. His men pressed on furiously with the attack however.

The ladders were placed against the hides of earth and we scaled them under a heavy fire from the Spaniards. We found the earth better stuff to encounter than stone, and though our poor captain fell in the breach whilst nobly leading on his men, we succeeded in forcing our way into the town, which was soon filled with the reinforcements that followed us. We drove the enemy from all the batteries, and massacred with sword and bayonet all whom we found carrying arms.[15]

The ramparts were now crowded with British soldiers who dropped the twelve feet from the breach into the town, the streets of which were defended by brass field pieces whilst muskets opened fire from the windows and tops of every house. The British troops charged into the town and some turned to their left and captured all the batteries as far as Fort St. Philip. At this point Colonel Vassal, of the 38th, fell, his leg shattered by grape shot, but he continued to cheer on his men as he lay dying upon the ground. His men rushed on, clearing the streets with fixed bayonets, overturning the Spanish guns as they went.

Meanwhile, the 40th Regiment had advanced to the walls in support of the stormers but they too could not find the breach and suffered heavily as they twice passed through the fire of the batteries whilst searching for it. Eventually it was pointed out to them by Lieutenant Harry Smith, the future Sir Harry Smith:

Most of the men fell, and many were wounded by each other's bayonets. When the head of the column entered the breach, the main body lost its communications or was checked by the tremendous fire. Perceiving the delay, I went back and conducted the column to the breach, when the place was immediately taken.[16]

The 87th Regiment was still waiting near the North Gate and grew impatient, listening to the main attack in progress at the breach. The men quickly grew tired of waiting for their comrades to open it for them and unable to restrain themselves any longer they scaled the walls and forced open the gate themselves, after which they poured into the town to join in the attack. During the assault a live shell landed next to a company of the 40th Regiment and was sure to do great damage if it exploded. At once, Sergeant William Luxton, regardless of the danger to himself, picked it up and threw it away whereupon it exploded without causing any casualties. Luxton later received a medal for his brave conduct.

By daylight most of the town was in British hands but there was still a detachment of Spanish troops holding out inside the Citadel. Auchmuty sent a flag of truce to their general ordering him to give up the place but the general refused. It was then left to some riflemen who scaled the towers of the cathedral, which overlooked the Citadel, to put an end to their resistance:

...three or four riflemen were placed on a tower sufficiently high and near to the Citadel for the purpose of, if possible, picking out the general and shooting him. This was soon effected, for on his appearing for a walk on the ramparts in his full uniform, one of the men shot him dead: and when the Spaniards found that they had lost their commander, they soon became disheartened, and lowering the drawbridge, came out of the Citadel and gave themselves up. Part of our troops immediately took possession, pulling down the Spanish colours and hoisting the English flag from the town and Citadel in their stead.[17]

At half-past eight the town surrendered and there followed a certain amount of disorder, although it was not very widespread. In fact, shortly afterwards the townspeople were able to walk about the streets as if nothing had happened. As soon as the town had fallen Lieutenant Milne took a party of men and set out in some armed launches to secure the surrender of the island of Ratones along with its guns and its small garrison of seventy.

The Spanish losses in the assault were severe and were estimated at over 3,000 killed, wounded and taken prisoner. The remainder of the garrison managed to escape across the harbour and slipped past the British in small boats. The British themselves did not get off lightly either, losing six officers and 110 men killed with twenty-one officers and 258 men wounded. The heaviest of these casualties occurred amongst the Light Battalion, who suffered sixty-three killed and eighty-four wounded out of a strength of only four or five companies, and the 38th Regiment who suffered twenty-seven killed and 121 wounded.

Most of the British casualties were sustained by the troops trying to find the breach at the foot of the walls in the face of a galling fire. The most notable of these casualties were Brownrigg and Vassal, whom Auchmuty could ill afford to lose. Such capable officers as these would be much needed in the second attack on Buenos Aires. The high casualty figures on both sides also bear testimony to the intensity of the struggle for Montevideo, the capture of which was vital to the whole campaign in the Rio de la Plata.

With Montevideo lost Sobremonte retired with his cavalry to Rosario, near Colonia. The news of the fall of the town reached Buenos Aires on 6 February and soon afterwards the people began to gather at the Cabildo, not only to hear the news from Montevideo but also to clamour once again for the deposition of the viceroy, whose behaviour during the siege was received by them with dismay and anger. Following the meeting a statement was issued by the Cabildo, part of the text of which read:

Let him be removed and entirely withdrawn, let his person be secured so that he shall neither cause embarrassment nor inconvenience.[18]

Following this the Cabildo, presided over by Alzaga, called a meeting on 10 February, composed of the military commanders, the tribunals and the principal inhabitants of the city, at which it was declared that:

...the Marquis de Sobremonte is suspended from the position of Viceroy, Governor and Captain General, that his person shall be secured and his papers taken possession of, the Audience exercising authority, until the pleasure of the King be known.[19]

As a result of this declaration two members of the Cabildo, supported by two or three companies of infantry and one of cavalry, crossed to Banda Oriental and arrested the Marquis and brought him back to Buenos Aires from where he was finally sent to Spain.

In all, the capture of Montevideo was a great success for Auchmuty, not only from the point of view of it being a successful military operation but because it gave the British a strong, secure base from which they could conduct the forthcoming operation against Buenos Aires.

V

Whitelocke

News of the capture of Montevideo by Auchmuty slowly began to filter through to the British prisoners held by the Spaniards in various parts of the colony, giving them some cause for hope, reassuring them that there was still a British army nearby and that freedom might be near at hand.

This morning we were informed that Montevideo was certainly in possession of the English, having been taken by assault, but on what day or night there does not seem to be any correctness. They also say that a reinforcement is arrived in the river, no certainty as to numbers. They also state that 6,000 English have left Montevideo for the capital [Buenos Aires], but the principal merchants have sent to offer terms, and the Creoles are determined not to fight against the English. How far this latter part is true time only will discover, for there is little or no credit to be given to their reports. [1]

Not all was discontent amongst the prisoners, however. In fact, there had been many desertions amongst them, particularly the Roman Catholics who, finding themselves in a strict catholic country, found the temptation of the land too great and so deserted to the enemy. There were fewer amongst the 71st Regiment which had formed the bulk of Beresford's force, only thirty-six in fact, which says a lot for their discipline, but amongst the sailors and the St. Helena Regiment the proportion was very large, many of the deserters later joining the patriotic armies during the wars of independence to fight against Spain.

Judging from the accounts written by British officers, they had been having a relatively enjoyable time. They played cricket, had gone shooting, had visited cattle ranches and were generally warmly received wherever they went. They had been given parole by their captors but with the fall of Montevideo they were moved deeper into the provinces, travelling in a convoy of wagons to Salta and then over the Los Condones to the Calamuchita Valley where most of them stayed either at San Ignacio or Santa Rosa.

When the news of the British triumph at Montevideo reached them they believed it would only be a matter of time before British troops were once again masters of Buenos Aires, after which they would all be released. Many of the local people realised this and fearing possible reprisals asked the prisoners for certificates stating that they had been fairly treated by them. Also, a Captain Martinez arrived at Santa Rosa to take away the parole book from Captain Gillespie who had been in charge of the Spanish prisoners taken during Beresford's capture of Buenos Aires. In the book were the signatures of the Spanish officers who had sworn never to take up arms against the British. Possibly Martinez intended to destroy the proof which the British government would be able to produce should they break their parole, which many of them had and would do. Gillespie had buried the book, however, and when he was freed later on he took it back with him to England.

As the officers moved deeper inland they began to find things a little less enjoyable. According to the accounts left to us, the majority were well treated and had little reason to complain but there were some incidents involving attacks on isolated British officers, usually whilst out on hunting trips or out riding. One incident involved Pack and Lieutenant Ogilvie:

> Ogilvie was dangerously wounded by a ball fired from a pistol, which had entered at his back and gone through his shoulder-blade and supposed to have touched his lung. This was committed by a villain who had enticed him and Lieutenant Pack out of the town, informing him that a person had arrived from Buenos Aires with letters and was afraid to enter the town. When they got about two miles off they began to get suspicious, and therefore turned about to go home. The scoundrel immediately attempted to lasso the colonel, who twice extricated himself, and Ogilvie did the same once. Not succeeding in this he rode up close to Ogilvie and discharged his pistol close to his back.[2]

These lassos were commonly used by the gauchos to catch horses but since beginning of the British invasion had come in useful in catching British soldiers also. Pococke was told one day of:

> ...a shocking murder that was committed by some villain or villains on the body of one of the officer's servants at Capel, whom he or they caught coming from a house in the same village on his way home. The poor fellow was secured by a lasso, and dragged a considerable

way. His throat was afterwards cut from ear to ear. This lasso is made from plaited strips of green hide, about the size of a coach whip, and in length from thirty to sixty feet, having a noose at one end. They throw at horses with wonderful dexterity and immediately the object of their pursuit is secured they gallop up at full speed, with the other end of the lasso fastened to the horse's saddle.[3]

The most notable of the British prisoners was, of course, Beresford who, along with other British officers, had sworn never again to take up arms against the colonists of the Rio de la Plata. Beresford had been spending his captivity in the village of Lujan, where seems to have passed most of his time holding receptions and organising shooting parties. With the arrival of British reinforcements, however, the Spaniards decided to move him and his colleagues away from Lujan, deeper into the interior of the country.

Shortly before he departed Beresford met two men, Saturnino Rodriguez Pina, a colonial born, and Aniceto Padilla, a Bolivian. Both were ardent opponents of Spanish rule. They found Beresford a staunch supporter of their ideas and agreed to help him escape so that he might in turn help their cause. Pina, who was in charge of the prisoners' supplies, had access to their quarters but the success of the plan depended on them being able to avoid detection by the ever watchful Martin de Alzaga, now the mayor of Buenos Aires.

Pina visited Alzaga and told him that Padilla had asked him to join in a plot by the leading residents and the British. This, in fact, was just a ploy to get Alzaga to grant Pina a free pass to help him uncover the alleged conspiracy. Alzaga fell for the story and granted Pina complete freedom of movement. This allowed him to obtain horses and disguises for Beresford and for Pack, whom the British general had also asked to be freed. When Pina and Padilla reached Lujan, however, they were told that all British prisoners, including Pack and Beresford, had been moved to Catamarca. Immediately the two set off after them. Beresford later recalled the episode:

Near Arrecifes, forty leagues from Buenos Aires, two Spanish officers (one Senor Liniers' secretary) came to me under the pretence of a mission from him, proposing to take me to the British Army at Montevideo, as by assisting my escape they were acting for the good of the country (they were both South Americans) and according to the wishes of the principal inhabitants of Buenos Aires. After much consideration, and fully aware that our commanders must be ignorant, as I myself had been, of the real state of affairs, and would run the chance that befell me of being deceived and betrayed, I determined to hazard every personal risk for what I considered to be of the utmost consequence to my country.[4]

Beresford and Pack were then sent to Buenos Aires where they were forced to hide for three days. They were then able to make their escape on board a small Portuguese trawler. By chance the trawler met H.M.S. *Charwel,l* a little below Ensenada, which took them the rest of the way to Montevideo, which they reached on 25 February. On his arrival in Montevideo Beresford was asked by Auchmuty to assume command of the army, using his local knowledge of the people generally and personally, and because of the knowledge gained during his spell in captivity. Beresford declined, however, saying that he thought Auchmuty quite capable of command. He added that it was best if he returned to England to report to the government and tell them exactly what had happened. Therefore, Auchmuty remained in command whilst Beresford sailed home to England. Pack, however, decided to stay, a decision which later almost cost him his life.

The story of the campaign in the Rio de la Plata now reached a significant point with an event not in South America but in London, for with Craufurd's reinforcements hopefully making their way to the Rio de la Plata the build up of British troops there seemed to the government to warrant the appointment of a new commander-in-chief to take command of the whole force. Auchmuty had achieved a great success with the capture of Montevideo but the news of this event had not yet reached London and as this was his first independent command he was passed over, as was Craufurd who was considered to be too junior an officer to succeed Auchmuty. The choice, therefore, made by the government in London was Lieutenant-General John Whitelocke, chosen mainly on the recommendation of the Duke of York. It was a poor choice.

Born in 1757, Whitelocke spent his early years at Lochee's military academy at Chelsea. At the end of 1778 he obtained a commission as an ensign in the 14th Foot and within two years had risen to the rank of lieutenant. In 1782 he left for Jamaica with his regiment and there married a daughter of William Lewis of that country. Another of the daughters married a brother officer, afterwards Sir Robert Brownrigg, who became military secretary and quartermaster-general and it was through him that Whitelocke enjoyed some influence. He obtained a company in the 36th Foot in 1784 and a majority in one of the newly raised battalions of the 60th in 1788. He went with it to the West Indies and in 1791 became lieutenant-colonel of the 13th Foot stationed in Jamaica. Over the next couple of years he saw active service in the islands against the French and served with some credit, particularly in the attack on Port-au-Prince. He continued to rise and by 30 October 1805, was lieutenant-general. He knew his profession well and there seems to have been little disagreement over his appointment as commander in South America. He did, however, possess one or two characteristics which earned him some measure of contempt from those serving beneath him:

His most objectionable characteristic seems to have been arrogant but spasmodic self-confidence, with an affection of coarse speech and manners which he conceived to be soldierlike bluntness, but which often degenerated into mere rudeness towards some of his inferiors and familiar obscenity towards others. He stooped to court the favour of the rank and file by affected use of their phrases, with the inevitable result that he earned only their thorough contempt. The inference is that he sought popularity with the lower ranks of the Army because he was unable to gain the respect of the higher.[5]

Nevertheless, Whitelocke was chosen along with Major-General Leveson-Gower who would act as his second-in-command. He was to take with him to the Rio de la Plata a battalion of the 89th Regiment, a battery of Horse Artillery and a draft of recruits for some various other units, in all about 1,800 men. His orders simply stated that he was to capture Buenos Aires and if successful was to install himself as governor with a salary of £4000 per year which was to be drawn from provincial revenues. At the end of March 1807, suitably briefed and confident of success, Whitelocke sailed for South America aboard the frigate *Thisbe*.

In Montevideo, meanwhile, Auchmuty was trying to restore an air of normality to the town. William Lawrence wrote:

Now that we had possession of a fine town, we could lie up comfortably, only having to put out three or four hundred men on picket round the walls and see that the gates of the town were closed every night at sunset and not opened till daylight in the morning, and then feeling that we could make ourselves quite at home. The inhabitants were meanwhile not altogether deprived of their livelihood, as our general issued a proclamation that they should open their shops and carry on their business as usual: and if any declined to open, he was kind enough to send parties to do it for them.[6]

Despite Auchmuty's best efforts to placate the population, the British had not been long in Montevideo when a plot to blow up the Government House, where Auchmuty and his staff were quartered, was discovered. The culprits of the alleged plot were found and condemned to be hanged. A scaffold was erected in the Plaza Matriz and the sentence read to a silent population but at the last moment Auchmuty stepped forward and pardoned the condemned men and consequently an air of friendship developed between the British and the population.

As the people of Montevideo settled down to resume as near a normal life as was possible in a town under occupation Auchmuty decided to publish a newspaper which he hoped would be an example of Britain's future commitment to the place. The newspaper, called the *Estella del*

Sur, or 'Star of the South', was printed in English and Spanish and was edited by a Mr. Bradford, the Spanish translator being Aniceto Padilla, the same man who had recently aided Pina in helping Beresford to escape from Buenos Aires. The newspaper was used by the British to point out the misery and damage caused to the colonists by the despotic nature of Spain's commercial policies compared with the freedom and commercial expansion which would ensue under British protection. This last statement was partly true because there had indeed been a marked increase in trade throughout the country following the arrival of an abundance of goods from Britain, with articles being sold at very cheap prices. All this was mainly due to Popham's circulars and also to the fact that with such an unstable political climate in Europe many articles had previously been hard to come by.

Aside from the problems of trying to win over the people of Montevideo to British protection Auchmuty was still dogged by problems within his own army, the greatest of which was desertion. As with the British troops being held prisoner on the other side of the Rio de la Plata the soldiers occupying Montevideo found the country not at all unpleasant and were tempted to desert not only by the pleasures of the land but also by the money offered to them by the local people who hoped to lure them away to join their own army.

> ...a sergeant and corporal of the Spanish army came in disguise and tried to enlist any of our men who would join their service, and unfortunately a sergeant named Goodfellow, one of my own regiment, accepted their proposals, tempted by the heavy bounty they offered. Another case of desertion was that of an officer's servant, who went away with the greater part of his master's clothes, taking with him likewise a Spanish lady; he was lucky enough to get off safe, and nothing was heard of him afterwards.[7]

Indeed, Whitelocke himself was later to notice this disturbing trend and in a letter written soon after he arrived in Montevideo said:

> Upwards of 170 men had gone over to the enemy previous to my arrival to Montevideo, and some since; the more the soldiers become acquainted with the plenty the country affords and the easy means of acquiring it, the greater would be the evil, as the temptation is irresistible to the common mind, beyond the calculation of those acquainted with the locality.[8]

Auchmuty hoped his men would take their minds off of the temptations offered to them by the country if they were kept busy, and knowing that it would only be a matter of time before a second attack would have to be made on Buenos Aires he busied his men making preparations. In the meantime he decided to strengthen his own position by sending Pack up river to garrison the strategically important post of Colonia de Sacramento, it being the nearest place to Buenos Aires on the opposite side of the river.

Pack sailed with 54 men of the 9th Light Dragoons, six companies of the 40th Regiment, three companies of light infantry and three companies of the 95th, about 1,100 men in all with two guns. Amongst the force which landed at Colonia on March 5th was William Lawrence:

> We landed with ease, and the enemy retreated out of the place after firing a few shots, leaving it in our hands, so that we again found ourselves for a time in uncomfortable quarters. We placed pickets of two or three hundred men round the place, and placed a chevaux-de-frise in the gate, formed of very sharp and pointed swords stuck very thickly into a beam which was made to turn on its axis ... Duty at this place was rather hard, owing to there being so few of us, and such a number on picket or at work building some batteries for our better protection.[9]

The Spanish units hovering in the area made frequent shows against the small garrison but with little success. Around midnight on 20 March, however, some of them moved forward and drove in the British piquets.

> One particular night a column of Spaniards which had crossed the river from Buenos Aires stormed this post, and were near carrying it by surprise had it not been for Scott and his guard of Riflemen, who most bravely defended the breach until the troops got under arms. The enemy were not pursued, as their numbers were not known and the night was dark.[10]

The Spaniards had been repulsed but it would not be long before they would try again.

On the evening of 10 May, and after a voyage of nine weeks, the frigate *Thisbe* sailed into Montevideo with Whitelocke on board. He wasted little time in asserting his authority. In fact, his arrival came as something of a surprise to Auchmuty who was told by the new commander-in-chief that in future he (Auchmuty) would consult with Gower on all military matters.

Before he could do so, however, Whitelocke assumed complete command over the troops and subsequently issued a stream of orders. From that day until just a few days before the army embarked for Buenos Aires Auchmuty had no particular command or influence with the troops at headquarters at all except twice when the men were under arms.

Auchmuty, the victor of Montevideo, was certainly less than happy with this treatment.

Upon his arrival, Whitelocke found that the troops under Craufurd had not yet arrived and so decided to wait before moving against Buenos Aires. He concentrated instead on securing his own position and on making preparations for the coming assault. He could not afford to wait too long, however, for the rainy season was due any day and he knew that once Craufurd did arrive he would have to turn his attention quickly to Buenos Aires or run the risk of being held up in Montevideo until the weather improved, which might take some months. Even as he contemplated this the weather grew worse:

> It was the middle of winter at Montevideo; the nights were frosty, with now and then a little snow, and great showers of hail as large as beans. In the day dreadful rains deluged all around. We had sometimes thunder and lightening. One particular night in particular the whole earth seemed one continual blaze. The mountain on the side of which the town is built re-echoed the thunder, as if it would rend in pieces. The whole inhabitants flocked to the churches or kneeled in the streets.[11]

One of the greatest problems facing the British was the lack of good horses for the cavalry and artillery, those currently in service being of a poor quality, quickly breaking down under the work load required from them. They also lacked sufficient forage, it being mid-winter, a time when little nourishment was to be obtained from the native grass. Consequently, Whitelocke ordered Brigadier-General Lumley to go up country in order to procure horses from the outlying areas where the British still had posts. Lumley explained to Whitelocke that it would be easier for him to buy horses from the local people, adding that he should be able to obtain good horses for around six dollars apiece. Lumley described the local horses already in service with the British:

> I must remark, that the horses in themselves are exceedingly clever horses as I ever saw in any country, this country (England) excepted. I think the cavalry might be mounted as well in that country as in this for that money; but the total want of dry food, corn and hay, upon our first arrival there, rendered them useless in a very few days.[12]

On 20 May, Lumley set off and soon reached a small village called L'Espados before stopping a few days at Connelans.

> Upon my arrival at Connelans, I found the large rivers that lay before it, where I intended to pass over with some detachments to procure

horses, or to have horses sent over to me, exceedingly overflowed earlier in the year than usual. The light troops of the enemy, *banditti* as we called them, had increased in number in all parts of the border of those rivers, and had deterred people with whom I had had communication from bringing down horses.[13]

Lumley could only cross these rivers with the support of a reinforcement which he duly requested and which arrived on 24 May. Along with the reinforcement, however, there arrived orders forbidding him to take any risks in order to preserve the troops for 'other purposes'. Consequently, Lumley felt unable to cross as it could only be passed by fords which were so deep that the horses had to swim across or be carried in small boats which were capable of ferrying just a few at a time. Faced with these problems Lumley thought it best to return to Montevideo with the hundred or so horses he had obtained at Connelans. On his arrival in the town he reported to Whitelocke who criticised him for not procuring a greater number and for fixing the price at six dollars. Lumley replied by saying that he could call upon the Cabildo of Montevideo to send out and collect horses in the same way as they had done for the King of Spain. The order went out on 1 June and four days later five hundred horses were brought in, a number of which were taken for the artillery and about 160 for the 17th Light Dragoons, the rest of the cavalry having to remain dismounted. The quality of the horses, however, left a lot to be desired, particularly of those sent to the artillery, and this factor would be a significant handicap to the British throughout the rest of the campaign.

On 30 May Whitelocke received some good news with the sighting in the mouth of the Rio de la Plata of Craufurd's reinforcements after a long and arduous journey. Even so, it was to be another two weeks before Craufurd finally reached the port of Montevideo owing to fogs and bad winds.

At Colonia, meanwhile, Spanish forces had been gathering to attack Pack's small garrison. On 8 June he learned that a Spanish force under General Elio had assembled at San Pedro, twelve miles away, and resolved at once to move against them, marching at 3 o'clock the next morning with a force of about a thousand men. Amongst them was William Lawrence:

We were called under arms at midnight and supplied with half a pound of beef for each man; the order then being given to return to our lodgings for two hours, and at the end of that time to fall in again. A little after two in the morning we left the town with an Indian for our guide ... we were on our way to fight some Spaniards.[14]

Arriving at San Pedro at seven o'clock in the morning, Pack found the Spaniards, who numbered about two thousand, strongly posted on a small hill with their front and flanks secured by a deep and marshy river, over which there was only one ford, and that was defended by four 6-pounders and two howitzers. Their cavalry formed a right angle with the right of their infantry and they had seven guns on their left. Pack decided to attack at once, extending three companies of the 95th along the river to cover the rest of the British infantry who crossed waist deep through the narrow ford under fire from the Spanish guns before forming up on the other side. Lawrence described the action:

> We found a river in our way; fortunately it was not very deep, so we waded through it under a heavy fire from the Spanish cannon, which killed two of our men whilst in the act of crossing; and as soon as we were over we formed line and advanced towards the enemy, who lay on some fine rising ground in our front. They had some few pieces of cannon with them and opened the first fire with both cannon and musketry, but every shot seemed to rise over our heads, and I don't think that volley killed a single man.[15]

The British troops advanced to attack without firing a shot and on seeing their resolute approach the Spanish cavalry turned and fled almost immediately. The Spanish infantry stood firm, however, but when the British got within thirty yards of them they could bear the strain no longer and they too turned and fled in disorder and were pursued with great slaughter. The Spaniards left one hundred and twenty of their men lying dead on the field with as many wounded. Over a hundred prisoners were taken along with a flag, eight guns, tents and stores and a great deal of ammunition, as well as:

> ...a nice breakfast cooking for us in the shape of fouls, geese, turkeys, beef, rice, and calavancos, (though the latter were too warm with cayenne pepper and garlic) all of which the enemy had to leave in his hurry and which came in very acceptably at the end of a long march.[16]

British losses in the action were forty-eight killed and wounded, including Major Gardiner, of the 95th, and fourteen of his men who were wounded, some badly, when an ammunition wagon exploded. Pack afterwards reckoned that had he been able to get both his artillery and cavalry across the river he would have been able to destroy almost the entire enemy force. After the action he returned to Colonia whilst General Elio, his reputation as a fearless leader somewhat tarnished, left the area altogether and returned with his men to Buenos Aires.

Shortly after Pack had returned to Colonia another small British outpost came under threat. This post was the village of Connelans which was held by a small British garrison under Backhouse. The village had been besieged by squads of Spanish cavalry which were active in that part of the country, and on 11 June Backhouse was summoned to surrender the village to them or risk facing an attack by about fourteen hundred men. Backhouse ignored the threats but thought it prudent to retire from the place and withdrew to Montevideo, meeting on the way Colonel Mahon, of the 9th Light Dragoons, who had been sent with five hundred men to support him, and together they returned safely to Montevideo which they reached on 14 June.

14 June also saw the arrival in Montevideo, finally, of Admiral Murray and the British reinforcements under Craufurd. We last saw this force on 26 April, sailing from St. Helena, and by the time the last of the transports arrived in Montevideo some of the troops had been aboard ship for almost nine months. In fact, some of them had been aboard ship even longer. For instance, five companies of the 95th had embarked on 26 July of the previous year at Gravesend from where they sailed down to Falmouth to join the rest of the British force destined for South America. These five companies, therefore, had been aboard ship for almost eleven months and were hardly in the best condition to fight a campaign.

The day after Craufurd's arrival Whitelocke invited him to join him on an inspection of the fortifications of Montevideo and on returning through the town Whitelocke made a prophetic observation which Craufurd later recalled:

> ...in returning through the town he [Whitelocke] desired me to notice the peculiar construction of the houses, their flat roofs surrounded by parapet walls, and other circumstances, which, as he observed, rendered them peculiarly favourable for defence, and added, that he would certainly not expose his troops to so unequal a contest, as that in which they would be engaged, if led into so large a town as Buenos Aires, all the inhabitants of which were prepared for its defence, and the houses of which were similarly constructed to those which he then pointed out to me.[17]

In three weeks' time, however, Whitelocke would do just that. In the meantime, Craufurd's arrival meant that there were now over ten thousand British troops in the Rio de la Plata and Whitelocke knew that with the rainy season at hand he could not delay the assault on Buenos Aires any longer than was necessary. There were several reasons for attacking without delay. Not least if the attack was postponed until after the rainy season the inhabitants of Buenos Aires would have the opportunity of turning the city into a heavily fortified place.

There was also the problem of keeping the British troops fed for an indefinite period of time, bearing in mind that there was already a shortage of flour in Montevideo. However, Pack, who had after all been in the country longer than anyone, thought it best to wait as it would give Craufurd's men a chance to recover from their voyage. These men had been cooped up for many months and were sure to be in a weak state and certainly unfit to embark upon a campaign such as that against Buenos Aires. Indeed, it is much to their credit that they were to behave as well as they did, given the circumstances.

Whitelocke, however, decided he could wait no longer and went ahead with his plan to attack the city, hoping that the rains might at least hold off until his army reached it. Having decided upon this course Whitelocke ordered his assistant quartermaster-general, Richard Bourke, to sail up the river to look for a suitable landing place on the south side of the river.

> That evening I went on board the Fly sloop and proceeded the next day up the river with Captain Thompson. We examined upon that day and the succeeding days, a considerable extent of the coast from at least sixty miles to the eastward of the Ensenada de Barragon, as far as six or seven miles to the westward of Buenos Aires; the result of which examination was, that we believed that there was no place where the troops could be landed under cover of the smallest ships of war, excepting at the Ensenada de Barragon.[18]

Navigation proved hazardous above Buenos Aires owing to the number of shoals, the fogs and other difficulties. Point de Quilmes, where Beresford had landed, was also considered but further reconnaissance showed that the Spaniards had constructed a battery there to thwart any future enemy landings. Thus it was decided that the landings would indeed take place at Ensenada de Barragon.

With the place of disembarkation decided upon, preparations for the expedition were stepped up and the harbour of Montevideo so crowded with shipping that it bore the appearance of 'a winter forest.' One last point remained, however. A decision still had to be made with regard to the small garrison under Pack at Colonia. Whitelocke was still unsure whether to leave the men there as an advanced base of operations, Colonia being directly opposite Buenos Aires, or abandon it altogether.

Eventually he despatched Gower with orders to bring away the garrison and either leave a small number of troops there to hold the place or withdraw completely. Whitelocke left the decision to Gower who later recalled:

> Lieutenant-General Whitelocke left it discretionary with me to leave a small force on shore if I found, from the reports which I collected on my arrival there, that they would have been left in any tolerable degree of security. Finding, from the reports which I collected, that

any considerable diminution of the number of troops at Colonia
would risk the loss of any detachment that might be left, I embarked
the whole.[19]

After breaking up the works and destroying the guns, therefore, Gower
re-embarked the whole garrison and returned to join the rest of the army
by which time it had embarked aboard the transports. Whitelocke divided
his force into four brigades with Craufurd, Auchmuty, Lumley and Mahon
each taking command of one of them. The 89th Regiment, which had
sailed from England at the same time as Whitelocke, along with a further
500 recruits for the various other regiments as well as a troop of horse
artillery, had not yet arrived. Apart from the troops who were to embark
upon the campaign against Buenos Aires Whitelocke set aside a garrison
of 1,353 men under Colonel Browne, of the 40th Regiment, who were to
remain in Montevideo. These consisted of the 47th regiment, two companies of the 38th, a few detachments of the 20th and 21st Light Dragoons,
some marines and a locally raised militia made up of merchants and other
British subjects, about four hundred strong, who underwent a course
of drilling so as to be ready to assist in the defence of the works in
the event of an attack on the town after the main army had departed
for Buenos Aires. This unit was called the Royal British South American
Militia.

The decision to leave behind the 47th Regiment and the two companies
of the 38th was puzzling since they were all tried and trusted and were
experienced on active service. They were certainly too valuable to the
expedition to be left behind kicking their heels in frustration as a garrison.
The same went for the seasoned detachments of the 20th and 21st Light
Dragoons. Whitelocke could have left behind in Montevideo the 88th and
36th regiments, both of which had been cooped up aboard ship for about
nine months, and the dismounted squadrons of the 6th Dragoon Guards
who would be forced to fight on foot in their clumsy great cavalry boots.
Nevertheless, Whitelocke had made up his mind and the embarkation
began.

The troops were embarked aboard ships with provisions for ten thousand men for twenty-one days. Twenty-eight guns consisting of three
24-pounders, three 12-pounders, eight 6-pounders, five 4-pounders, two
St. Helena 3-pounders, two 12-inch mortars and five howitzers were also
embarked. There were two hundred rounds of ammunition for each gun
to be carried in eight carriages, and the same number of carriages was
also to transport the 2,671,000 musket ball cartridges and 20,000 carbine
cartridges. In addition were embarked 40,000 rounds of rifle ball ammunition, exclusive of 350 rounds per man belonging to the 95th Rifles.

Bad weather delayed the departure of the troops and it was not until 17
June that Auchmuty and his brigade were eventually able to get under-

way, anchoring off Colonia where the whole fleet of transports was to rendezvous on the 24th. Here, two days later, they were met by the ships bringing Gower with Pack's garrison from Colonia and together the whole fleet set sail for Ensenada de Barragon. The campaign had begun.

VI

The March to Buenos Aires

The British fleet carrying the troops who were destined to attack Buenos Aires crossed the Rio de la Plata and arrived off Ensenada de Barragon at daylight on 28 June. The vessels carrying the Light Brigade, with the 87th Regiment as its support, weighed anchor at daylight and stood into a creek. At the entrance of the creek a gun-brig was moored with a signal flying for the number of feet of water, altering it as the tide rose and fell. As the ships carrying the rest of the troops neared shore a thick fog suddenly came down but they formed a chain and so avoided danger, and although two of them did collide no great harm was done.

The disembarkation started almost immediately with the Light Battalion and the 95th Rifles, both of which were ashore before the fog came down. This was not accomplished without difficulty, however, because the small transport ships could not get close in to the shore, owing to a long sand bar which obstructed the approach. Craufurd's Brigade had to wade a considerable distance to reach it. Fortunately, a channel was found through it which enabled the rest of the army to land relatively dry. Soon afterwards Gower began to advance inland with Craufurd's brigade along with the 38th and 87th Regiments and by one o'clock in the afternoon they had occupied some heights about four miles inland where they camped for the night.

The day after the landings the main body of the army began to advance inland only to discover to their dismay that between them and the heights, upon which ran the only passable road to Reduction, there lay a wet, swampy morass stretching for two miles. Whitelocke had failed to carry out any reconnaissance of the area around Ensenada or of the line of march, and it was only as the British troops advanced that the full extent of their task dawned upon them. The level of the country to a distance of between two and four miles inland was just over two feet above the level of the river and as it was the rainy season the ground had turned into a swamp and was almost entirely under water. This marshy land would have to be crossed before the army could gain the heights and the road to Reduction. From Reduction the road ran across another area of wet level ground before it crossed the Rio Chuelo by a small wooden bridge. This had been destroyed in June 1806 at the time of Beresford's landing but it had since been rebuilt.

The failure by Whitelocke to carry out any serious reconnaissance of the country through which he intended to advance would prove to be a great mistake and was something which would prove a great handicap to his men. This total lack of reconnaissance of the land between Ensenada and Buenos Aires was later confirmed by Lieutenant-Colonel Bourke at Whitelocke's trial, and although Bourke said he had been sent with Captain Thompson, of the *Fly*, to carry out a survey of the Rio de la Plata it had been for the purpose only of establishing a suitable landing place. This was deemed necessary in view of the fact that several batteries of guns had recently established by the Spaniards in the wake of the previous invasion by Beresford. When asked at the trial, Bourke confirmed that, other than the search for a suitable landing place, no other detailed survey of the land had been made. He was, however, aware of the marsh but claimed that information received led him to believe that wagons travelled freely across it:

> The whole of the information which we had received respecting this place, and the roads and country from thence to Buenos Aires, amounted I think to this: the distance from Ensenada to Reduction was sent to be about 20 miles, and from thence to Buenos Aires nine miles: that there were three different roads, one on the sands, one through the marsh, and the third upon the heights; the last was said to be the best: that in order to reach the heights some marshy grounds must be passed, through which the wagons and carts of the country commonly travelled.[1]

It is obvious from this statement that the true nature and extent of the problems posed by the marsh were unknown. There is also no doubt that further surveys should have been carried out and that to commit to a landing on the basis of such scant information was dangerous. It was to have a major bearing on the outcome of the campaign. Meanwhile, the British troops, already wearied by undaunted, pushed on:

> The country is almost all level and covered with long clover that reached to our waists, and large herds of bullocks and horses which seemed to run wild. The weather was very wet. For days I had not a dry article on my body. We crossed many morasses in our march, in

one of which I lost my shoes and was under the necessity of marching the rest of the way barefooted.[2]

As the British advance guard continued their march the swamp grew steadily worse under the trampling of hundreds of feet and it quickly turned into a sea of black liquid mud through which the main body of the army now plunged, the men stumbling and tripping over the plants and reeds that lay hidden in the water beneath their feet. They pushed on, nevertheless, with great effort and determination, pausing only to fish around in the water for a lost shoe or musket. Some of them even managed to joke about their condition, splashing around and laughing, whilst the 5th Regiment on landing had been loudly cheered when it captured a pig. In fact, the men of the 5th could consider themselves fortunate in being able to have procured some sort of food because large quantities of the men's food and water, carried by them in their haversacks, was soon rendered uneatable and useless by the mud and water.

In the meantime, Whitelocke had given orders for three days' rations of biscuits and spirits to be landed which was done the same day, the 29th, but problems soon arose over transportation. Many of the horses which had been landed in order to transport the supplies were unbroken. They would not carry their saddle packs and ran about in all directions. Many of them broke loose and were never recovered and as a consequence it was necessary to dismount sixty men of the 17th Light Dragoons, already hit by a lack of horses, in order to furnish the Commissariat with replacements. Eventually, eight tons of biscuit were landed and loaded up ready to be shipped forward to the army but only one ton actually reached the men, the rest being swallowed up or ruined in the swamp, whilst only a small quantity was re-embarked aboard the ships.

Equally as important to the troops, of course, was the rum supply and great efforts were made to bring it forward in mule carts. But once again these proved useless. The wheels stuck fast in the swamp and the carts could not be moved, the Commissariat being forced to stove in the casks and abandon them to sink in the swamp. It was all total confusion and despair.

The situation was just as dire for the artillery. They had managed to land sixteen guns but the mud was so thick that, although drawn by six horses instead of the usual four, five light pieces captured from the Spaniards had to be spiked and abandoned whilst the rest of the guns had to remain firmly stuck in the morass until late in the day when hundreds of marines and seamen hauled them out and dragged them up on to the heights.

By the end of 29 June the British army had struggled out of the morass and had reached the heights above Ensenada where it halted for the night on the ground occupied by Gower the night before. It had advanced barely six miles, had lost the greater part of its rations and had lost a number of horses and guns. In spite of the conditions the men themselves were in good spirits, although most were thoroughly exhausted. It was just as well that the landings had taken place without any opposition from Liniers' army, otherwise the situation may well have been totally disastrous. But although the British army had been able to land without opposition there were nevertheless some small enemy units in the area, mainly local irregulars, who were a constant nuisance:

> These men were chiefly country people, who are called 'paysanos' or 'camelocchios'; they are very expert at throwing a sort of leather noose over men, horses and cattle. Two officers were attacked by them, Lieutenants Lloyd, of the 17th Dragoons, and Robert Crosse, of the 36th Regiment. The former, with the noose over him, had the presence of mind to charge the fellow before he pulled him off his horse, he cut the rascal severely on the head, and thus escaped. The other officer had the noose thrown twice at him and was also fired at; the noose took his hat off the first time, and nearly carried away his sword the second, but he fortunately escaped. Two men of the 95th or Rifle Corps, were likewise attacked by a party of them, one had actually the noose about his head, when his companion shot the fellow, and saved his comrade's life. The other rising from the ground, had only time to get upon his legs when he beheld his brave preserver 'lassoed' also in a moment; he fired, and repaid the obligation by knocking the man off his horse, and saving the Rifleman, who was already half strangled. Captain Brooke, of the 5th, accompanied by a single dragoon, was also 'lassoed', but he had the presence of mind to fire his pistol, and make the fellow fly.[3]

William Lawrence also relates the story of three soldiers who were attacked whilst plundering some huts. Some locals fell upon them, lassoing two of them, dragging them off and killing them whilst the third managed to escape with a sabre wound. One of the British dead, a corporal, had his head cut off and stuck upon a pole: such were the perils of being a straggler.

Meanwhile, Whitelocke had ordered Gower to push forward and the latter complied by sending forward Craufurd's brigade with some light field pieces and some mounted dragoons. Lumley's brigade followed some three or four miles behind, the idea being that Craufurd should find fuel and shelter at the few farmhouses along the way. In doing this, however, the British columns became scattered and with the small number of mounted troops with them becoming fewer and fewer each day through exhaustion and collapse communication between the columns became extremely difficult. Also, in the event of an attack by the Spaniards the columns would be unable to support each other. Nevertheless, Gower pushed on for a few miles and then halted to await the main body of the army.

Whitelocke gave orders for his own men to resume their march at nine o'clock on the morning of 30 June but here arose the problem of provisions. The greater part of the troops' supply of bread, biscuit and spirit had been swallowed up during the march through the swamp, and of their own three days' rations some battalions, through faulty staff work, failed to receive any. This meant that with the nearest supplies two days distance away the men faced a march of at least a day without food. Fortunately, a flock of sheep was found and to some extent the army managed to feed itself. Even here though there was confusion, for Whitelocke had already fixed the hour to begin the march at nine o'clock, which was late enough itself, but on the acquisition of the sheep it was delayed even longer and in the delay and confusion during the distribution of the meat many of the men received nothing at all whilst some of those who did had no time to cook their food before they were ordered to resume the march.

When Whitelocke did eventually set off he left behind Mahon with four companies of the 40th Regiment and the 17th Light Dragoons, mounted and dismounted, to act as rearguard and as escort for the artillery, as the seamen and horses who had dragged the guns from the swamp were too exhausted to continue. The other troops also began to feel the strain, with the lack of food in particular taking its toll, particularly amongst Lumley's brigade, being unseasoned and mainly young troops. When the army halted on the evening of the 30th, Whitelocke's tired and hungry men had reached a point only five miles beyond the heights with Gower seven miles beyond that.

At last, on 1 July, Gower approached the village of Reduction, which was quickly occupied by the Light Brigade. Enemy resistance had been expected here but only a small body of horsemen showed themselves and these were quickly scattered by a single shot from a British gun. The occupation of Reduction proved a great morale booster for tired troops of the British vanguard as the lofty towers of the churches in Buenos Aires could now be seen clearly from it, and with their objective in sight they now began to feel that the campaign was actually getting somewhere.

> We now got sight of this capital; and the spirits of the troops were not
> a little cheered by a first view of the object which they expected to
> reward them most amply for all their toils and a tedious march.[4]

Whitelocke himself rode forward to Gower and urged him to push forward beyond the village to the Rio Chuelo in order to secure the bridge there, but he was able to march only another two or three miles before the marshy ground in front of him forced him to a standstill and he halted for the night where he was. The main body of the army, meanwhile, trudged wearily into Reduction. This meant that communication between them and the fleet could be resumed through Point de Quilmes, the scene of Beresford's landing in 1806, which cheered the men no end, for it meant that it was now possible for them to be supplied from the ships although again there were still two miles of swamp between Quilmes and Reduction over which everything would have to be carried.

Whitelocke decided to remain at Reduction the next day, 2 July, in order to send parties to Quilmes to fetch supplies landed from the ships and also to allow Mahon to bring forward the artillery, which was still some way in rear of the main body of the army. News of the halt came as a relief to the men who could now look forward to receiving a fresh supply of bread and spirits. Their joy, however, was short lived. It had been a miserable day and it had been raining heavily. At two o'clock in the morning Whitelocke, fearing that storms might prevent his men from crossing the Chuelo and eager to get his men into the suburbs of Buenos Aires and under shelter, changed his mind and decided instead to continue his march later that morning. Consequently, orders were sent forward to Gower instructing him to move forward with the vanguard of the army and cross the Chuelo using the first practicable ford above the bridge which was thought to be held by the enemy or destroyed, and then take up a position on the heights to the west of the capital. From here Gower was to make contact with the fleet and afterwards was to summon Liniers to surrender.

Whitelocke's order to march was carried to Gower by Quartermaster Bourke who was, to say the least, not happy with it. Nor was Gower. His men, in particular the 36th and 88th Regiments, were thoroughly exhausted and in need of food and rest. But an order was an order and Gower obeyed, giving Bourke a letter to deliver to Whitelocke in which he stated his intention to cross the Chuelo by either marching around its source or crossing by a ford higher up the river since the Passo Chico, mentioned by Whitelocke, was believed to be impracticable. Auchmuty, meanwhile, had protested strongly to the commander-in-chief, pointing out to him the exhausted state of the men and of the need to rest, adding that, judging by the amount of stragglers left behind in Reduction by Lumley's brigade, the vanguard must be in a worse condition still. Whitelocke would not be moved, however, and the order was given for the men to march at nine o'clock that morning.

One can imagine the anger of the British troops on hearing the order as they were all about to tuck into their first decent meal for days. Bullocks had been slaughtered and the meat cut up and distributed ready to be cooked, when all of a sudden the men were ordered to overturn their pots, put out the fires and be ready to march. The men were not even allowed to put the meat into their haversacks, and a vast quantity had to be thrown away and left to rot. Also, in order that they might be able to march quicker Whitelocke ordered the men to throw away their blankets and march with greatcoats only. All this, coming as it did amidst the pouring rain, did little for the men's morale.

In spite of protests from their officers the tired British troops were forced to resume their march leaving hundreds behind in Reduction, unable to go on any further, whilst Mahon was ordered to bring forward the rearguard to the village and await further instructions. At this point, however, we must leave the advancing British army in order to look at the movements of Liniers' army as it prepared to defend Buenos Aires.

Liniers had marched out of the capital on 1 July taking with him almost the entire garrison, some 6,937 men and 53 pieces of artillery, and had crossed the Rio Chuelo by the bridge which the British had themselves thought was already occupied by Liniers. This was not the case, however, and believing that the British themselves would attack him there Liniers, on 2 July, drew up his army to face the advancing British, placing Balbiani on the right, Elio in the centre and Velazco on the left. Gutierrez de la Concha commanded the reserve.

Ironically, Gower had no intention of crossing the Chuelo by the bridge as he had always assumed that it had either been destroyed or would be heavily defended by the Spaniards. Instead he had been trying to find a passable ford by which to cross. As Craufurd himself later recalled, 'the enemy had such bodies of cavalrymen between us and the bridge at the Rio Chuelo, that nothing but a considerable force could have approached it.'[5]

In fact, Gower had received reports that Liniers had set up strong batteries to defend the bridge and the Spanish position around it, and so the search for a ford across the river continued until suddenly the way across was somewhat fortuitously shown by the enemy themselves. This happened when Craufurd's brigade, which was as usual far out in front of Lumley's men, spotted a force of enemy cavalry who, on being quickly driven off, appeared to cross the Chuelo by the Passo Chico, a ford which the British had previously believed to be impassable. Consequently, Gower decided to follow suit and soon the men were plunging waist deep through the water to cross to the opposite bank.

> The men immediately dashed through the water which came about to their hips. Great was our joy at having gained this important pass; every individual was animated, the men cheered and could hardly be restrained from boisterous expressions of delight.[6]

> There was no enemy opposite, and it was instantly forded, being about four feet deep, and thirty yards over; its current was not rapid, and the bottom was a firm gravel. The ammunition wagon belonging to our three pounders was carried over on men's shoulders...over the obstacle we expected to have proved the most formidable on our march.[7]

The passage of the Rio Chuelo meant that the greatest obstacle in the way of the British march on Buenos Aires was now cleared and the way to the capital was open.

For Liniers and his army, the news of Gower's crossing came as a complete shock. There they were, drawn up in force and fully expecting an advance on the bridge, when they suddenly received the news that the British had simply marched around them leaving them outflanked and the city open. In fact, the city itself was protected by just a single battalion of *Patricios* along with the small garrison inside the Fortress. Liniers suddenly had a serious crisis on his hands and the fate of Buenos Aires hung in the balance. He had to act fast and despatched Velazco's column, of some 1,500 men in all with several guns, to intercept Gower and prevent him from entering the city, whilst Elio had orders to follow also, leaving another body of troops at the Rio Chuelo. Liniers himself rode with his escort and rejoined Velazco's column which marched through the suburbs of the city before reaching the open space of the Corrale del Miserere. Elio's column, however, lost its way and was unable to reach the place and returned instead to the city.

At the Corrale, Liniers, without really studying his position, hastily massed his troops facing west behind the hedges and ditches of some farmyards where they waited anxiously for the approaching British column. The British column itself crossed the ford at the Passo Chico at about three o'clock, by which time the men of Lumley's brigade were in a state of total exhaustion, many of them beginning to straggle in all directions. But Craufurd's men, although equally tired, pushed ahead and spotted a large body of the enemy hurrying from the bridge. These men were, in fact, Velazco's men who, realising they had been outflanked by Gower, were falling back on the city. Craufurd asked Gower for permission to pursue them to which the latter replied that he should go ahead, adding that he would support him with Lumley's brigade. Craufurd advanced and soon arrived at a house belonging to an American, William White, which lay about a mile to the west of the city.

By now Gower himself had joined Craufurd at the head of the Light Brigade and although the ground was covered with fences, hedges and gardens which made it impossible to see very far, both British commanders sensed that the enemy were very near although as yet unseen. The brigade passed through these obstacles and entered a large, open square which was in fact a slaughter yard. Here it halted in order to bring up eight field pieces whilst the men took the opportunity to grab some much needed rest. Suddenly, a single gun was heard and immediately a heavy fire of grape, round shot and musketry opened up on them from all round the square. The British troops were taken by surprise and for a moment fell back, huddling together seeking shelter from the enemy's fire. It was left to Gower to steady them with a few words before speaking to Craufurd who later recalled:

1. *Above left:* Francisco de Miranda

2. *Above right:* Sir Home Riggs Popham

3. *Above left:* The Marquis de Sobremonte

4. *Above right:* William Carr Beresford

5. British troops land at Quilmes in June 1806 before moving against Buenos Aires.

6. Beresford's troops enter the outskirts of Buenos Aires.

7. Another view of the British landings at Quilmes on 25 June 1806.

8. British troops at Lujan on 9 July 1806, taking possession of the treasure which had been taken there for safekeeping.

9. *Left:* La Reconquista. Spanish troops attack Beresford in the Plaza Mayor on 12 August 1806.

10. *Below:* La Reconquista. Beresford surrenders his sword to Santiago Liniers.

11. *Left:* A contemporary view of the town and citadel of Montevideo.

Opposite page, clockwise from top:
12. The storming of Montevideo on 3 February 1807.
13. Sir Samuel Auchmuty.
14. Robert Craufurd.

15. *Above left:* John Whitelocke.

16. *Above right:* Denis Pack.

17. *Above left:* Francisco Xavier de Elio.

18. *Above right:* Santiago Liniers.

19. *Above left:* Martin de Alzaga.

20. *Above right:* Juan Martin de Pueyrredon.

21. The death of Captain Renny, of the 40th Foot, at Montevideo.

22. *Top:* Another view of the attack on Montevideo, 3 February 1807.

23. *Middle left:* British soldiers on guard duty outside Montevideo in February 1807.

24. *Above right:* A contemporary view of British troops in Montevideo after its capture.

25. *Above:* Montevideo surrenders to Sir Samuel Auchmuty, 4 February 1807.

26. La Defensa. A column of British troops comes under attack from the rooftops on 6 July 1807.

27. Soldiers from the *Patricios* regiment attacking Craufurd's men in the church of Santa Domingo on 6 July 1807.

28. La Defensa. Whitelocke surrenders to Liniers on 6 July 1807.

29. Liniers' volunteer cavalry.

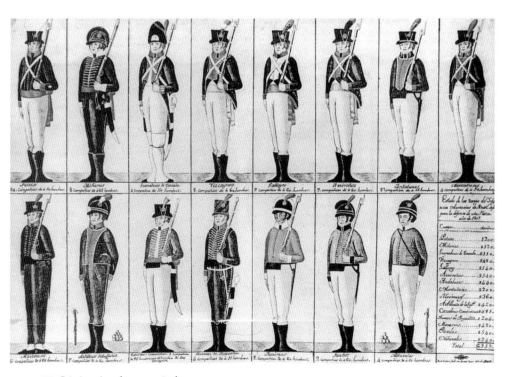

30. Liniers' volunteer infantry.

31. A trooper of the 1st Escuadron de Husares (Husares de Pueyrredon), part of Liniers' New Army.

32. A Miguelte. This regiment was clothed in red tunics, made from the jackets taken from the 71st Highlanders in 1806.

33. An officer of the Cazadores de Correntinos, a company of riflemen.

34. An officer of the *Patricios*, the most famous of Liniers' regiments.

35. An officer of the Cazadores de la Reyna (4th Husares).

36. A nonchalant officer of the 2nd Escuadron de Husares (Husares de Vivas).

37. An officer of the Tercio de Vizcainos.

38. Officer, Granaderos Provinciales.

39. Santiago Liniers is executed on 10 August 1810. It was a sad end for the man who, only two years before, had saved Buenos Aires from the British.

40. Whitelocke was lucky to escape execution after his showing at Buenos Aires. Here, the complaining ghost of Admiral Byng returns to remind Whitelocke how fortunate he was not to share a similar fate.

The ground was so extremely intricate and covered with peach orchards and high fences, that, although the enemy were at this time very near us, we certainly had not discovered them. The first indication which we had of their presence in force, was a shot fired from a gun at a distance just as General Gower and myself, with some of the staff officers, appeared upon the great road, upon which the column was then standing, and which road leads into the town by the slaughtering place called the Coral, which is the open space upon which the enemy's guns were placed. As soon as this gun was fired, General Gower said something to me, 'We must turn the right and left flank.' I understood this as an order to attack the enemy, and immediately obeyed.[8]

Craufurd wasted no time and immediately ordered forward the 95th Rifles and the Light Infantry companies who, with a great cheer, charged straight towards the Spanish guns. Craufurd again:

The enemy's fire for a very short time appeared to be that of rather a considerable body of infantry: but the light infantry and the 95th advanced so rapidly that they very soon gave way, leaving behind them twelve pieces of artillery. I pursued them about three quarters of a mile beyond the position on which they had been formed, nearby to the commencement of the town.[9]

Indeed, it had been a ferocious attack by the British troops who, after the tribulations of the last few days march, found someone upon whom to vent their anger. The sight of these fierce looking troops coming straight at them was too much for the Spaniards to bear. They abandoned their guns and fled in terror through the suburbs, pursued by Craufurd's men who ruthlessly bayoneted any stragglers they caught up with. The Spaniards lost sixty men killed and seventy made prisoners whilst Liniers himself managed to escape with his escort along with Velazco and four hundred other men. The Spanish commander had lost his artillery, had seen his force routed and was totally disheartened. He was left to roam the countryside with the few men he still had with him. He stayed that night at a small farm near La Chacarita, about a mile behind the British lines, where he spent, as he himself later put it, *la noche mas amarga de mi vida*, 'the most bitter night of my life.'[10]

The Spaniards had retreated in total disorder and were without leadership and it gave Craufurd a great opportunity to follow up his victory and enter right into the city to secure its capture. This would have brought the campaign to a swift and successful end. But at this point, with a golden opportunity staring the British right in the face, Gower ordered Craufurd to halt and return to the Corrale. 'It appeared to me,' Craufurd said later, at the moment advisable to follow the enemy into the town, and I desired the officer who brought me the order to request the General to allow me to do so. In answer I received a peremptory order to fall back to the Coral.[11]

To Craufurd the order seemed madness but for the Spaniards it meant that the defenceless city of Buenos Aires might yet be saved. As one historian later put it:

It is a curious commentary on the topsy-turvy nature of this whole campaign that, while Whitelocke was worrying himself into a needless frenzy of the fate of his advanced guard, that advanced guard was, with far more justification in fact, chafing angrily at the lost opportunity of entering Buenos Aires on the heels of the panic-stricken defenders.[12]

Lumley's brigade, meanwhile, had lost sight of the Light Brigade and many of his men, tired and hungry, began to drop down by the roadside. At the sound of firing a short way in front of them, however, Lumley began making frantic appeals to his men, urging them to make a greater effort to get forward to support their comrades. Many more of his men dropped out, unable to keep up as he pushed ahead following the sound of the gunfire.

The light was closing in, however, and it became impossible to find Craufurd's men in the dark and all trace of them was lost. For an hour or so Lumley tried to guide his brigade as best he could through the narrow lanes of the suburbs until, fortunately, he stumbled across the Light Brigade which had just returned from the pursuit of the defeated Spaniards. Here the two brigades camped for the night.

After marching about, up and down the lanes in the dark, we came to a plain almost close to the town, whose lamps we could plainly perceive. Here, amongst bullocks' heads and entrails, we found the Light Brigade drawn up; and here, with the customary precautions, we spent the night amidst rain, thunder, lightning and the yell of ten thousand dogs. This was actually the encamping ground of the enemy, and they kindly left us in possession of it; the men only standing to arms once in the night. At daylight the whole line stood to their arms, and found, to their great surprise, that they were in the suburbs.[13]

Whitelocke, with the main body of the army, wet, weary and grumbling, decided to camp that night, the 2nd, on some ground still some way short of the Rio Chuelo. He had received no information at all from Gower because communication between the different columns was still hampered by the persistent raids by small groups of enemy cavalry. Earlier on the 2nd, the commander-in-chief had spotted Gower and the vanguard making, he assumed, for the upper fords of the Chuelo but then he lost sight of them as they vanished from view. This was the point at which they forded the Passo Chico. 'We discovered,' said Whitelocke,

> that we had lost all traces of General Gower although our view from the ground was very extensive. It was four o'clock, approaching at that season to the close of the evening, when I was joined by Auchmuty from the rear, whose opinion immediately decided mine for halting that night, being in a vicinity of some large farms affording wood to dry the men and cook their victuals; the supply of cattle in a very extensive range of view.[14]

Los CondonesAt last, the men were indeed able to rest and eat. A few hours later Whitelocke heard the sound of gunfire coming from somewhere across the Chuelo which was, in fact, Gower's engagement at the Corrale, but it was not until the morning of the 3rd, just before daybreak, that he received Gower's report of the fight which was brought to him by the American, White, who had lived in the colony for some years and who knew the country well. Whitelocke's division resumed its march shortly afterwards:

> About 7 or sooner we moved off, 1st Brigade leading. General Whitelocke was rather bilious this morning and found much fault, amongst other things he called us 'a regiment of tailors'! …there was some trifling sniping, but we advanced about a mile or two without obstruction … Thinking that we should advance at once into the town, the leading regiments pushed on fast, which fell very heavily on the rear, and notwithstanding that we repeated the signal of our being overpressed, no alteration was made in the pace, and we were compelled to run uphill, though ankle-deep in a thick mud or clay, for a mile nearly. Our regiment left twenty or thirty on the road, the 5th many more, and every corps a few.[15]

The British army crossed the Chuelo by means of a narrow ford which they reached at about ten o'clock. The water here was deep and the troops waded across with water up to their armpits.

> I ought to have remarked that in crossing the river, the water was so high, that the men with difficulty got their ammunition safely over. How a young gentleman, Ensign Hopkins, got over I never learnt, he was a mere boy and very short.[16]

The British troops managed to cross safely, however, and by one o'clock the last man was over. Two hours later, the entire force, with the exception of Mahon's detachment, was at last re-united. The troops remained in this position throughout the rest of the day during which several minor skirmishes took place on the left, where a battalion company of the 36th and the 5th Regiments was placed. In one such skirmish a subaltern, with nine or ten men, drove a body of enemy horsemen one hundred and fifty strong nearly a mile from the lines killing two and wounding the officer who led them.

The British troops found most of the houses in the vicinity to be deserted, their former occupants having left as the invaders approached. The British troops who entered them were mainly looking for food and fuel. The occupants appeared to have left in a hurry, as one British soldier later recalled:

> everything was topsy-turvy; the boxes were lying open, covered with the richest clothes of all kinds; candles were seen lighted in every room, and horror seemed to hold uninterrupted reign, which was not at all broken in upon by the presence of the poor black slaves who were hiding about in the holes and corners.[17]

When Liniers marched out of Buenos Aires on 1 July with almost his entire army, the city had been left completely defenceless, save for a single battalion of *Patricios*. Since then the inhabitants had been living in a state of fear lest they should be attacked by the British army. The tension increased further with the arrival towards midnight of the force under Elio who brought with him the news of how the British had marched around the flank of Liniers' force at the Rio Chuelo. Elio added that whilst the divisions of Balbiani and de la Concha had remained on the opposite side of the river, Liniers had marched with Velazco to try and stop them entering the city. Unknown to everybody, however, was the fact that Liniers had been defeated at the Corrale, and just such a situation as the people had feared had now become a reality. The British army had reached the outskirts of the city, the Spaniards' leader was missing and with the troops routed the people were left with little hope, believing that it would be only a matter of time before the city was once again occupied by the British, this time with a larger force.

It was amidst this atmosphere of despair that Martin de Alzaga, mayor of Buenos Aires, took hold of the situation and found enough spirit to inspire the people to stand firm and prepare the city to resist the British attack. Defensive measures were quickly adopted and plans put into action with twenty-two ditches, four yards in depth and seven in width, being cut across the streets with one or two guns positioned in each. Alzaga traced a defensive line around the vicinity of the Fortress, the line extending to three or four squares in all directions from the Plaza Mayor, the entrances to which were blocked by guns. The way in which the city had been constructed, squares set at right angles to each other, meant that the Spanish guns could sweep the entire length of a street and so just a few guns would be capable of inflicting a great deal of damage on any invaders as the British, to their cost, were soon to find out.

The people laboured tirelessly throughout the night in an effort to complete the defences before the enemy attacked. Fortunately for them, Whitelocke's men were in such a state of fatigue that the British commander finally and somewhat belatedly ordered them to rest for the day. Thus, the work in Buenos Aires continued without interruption. The city's light contractor had been ordered to find as many lamps as possible to light up the main streets and keep them burning all night in order to bring some comfort to the tense inhabitants and when daylight broke on the morning of the 3rd Alzaga took stock of the situation to find that, astonishingly, all the defences, ditches and barricades had been completed.

As the first streaks of daylight began to filter through from the east, the troops defeated at the Corrale began to arrive in Buenos Aires bringing with them the news of Liniers' defeat. These were followed soon afterwards by the troops under De La Concha and Balbiani. These two divisions had been left behind by Liniers at the Rio Chuelo and with the departure of their leader they supposed the threat to Buenos Aires to be coming from the west. Therefore, with no enemy in sight Balbiani and De la Concha decided that it was no longer necessary to maintain their position and that they would march back to the city. The troops were already in a state of panic, however, as rumours had spread that Liniers had been defeated and that the British had already entered the city. They naturally feared for the safety of their families and soon it was a case of every man for himself as they fled on foot or on horse as fast as they could towards Buenos Aires and home.

Balbiani himself entered the city with only a thousand men but found, to his great relief, that the rumours were false and that the city was still safe. Liniers, meanwhile, was still at La Chacarita but on receiving the news that the British army was still at the Corrale he set off with his few remaining troops and marched towards the city which he entered about midday on 3 July and immediately set about organising his forces for the defence.

Liniers knew that it would be useless to try and face Whitelocke's trained British soldiers in the open field with a force of what amounted virtually to a militia, the more so since he knew that as a naval officer he lacked the necessary military experience needed by a field commander. His plan, therefore, was to take advantage of the natural defences which the construction of the city gave him. He would allow the British troops to penetrate deep into the city before launching his counter-attack. Having decided upon this he began to distribute and organise his troops.

As the centre of the defence he took the Fortress and an entrenched line which ran to the right from the Merced convent to the street in line with the San Miguel church, running along the Calle Suipacha leading south. This formed the front line. The line then passed down the Calle Potosi to the Calle del Peru, extending to the left and ending in front of the Santa Domingo church. On the extreme right was the Retiro, heavily defended, and the Plaza de Toros which brimmed with Spanish muskets.

Liniers placed his regular troops and a great number of the inhabitants of the city on the roofs and balconies of the houses and at the windows. The buildings around the Merced church were defended by the battalion of Arribenos, a company of the Corrientinos and the 3rd *Patricios*. The house of Serrada, at the northern angle of the line of defence, was occupied by a company of the 2nd *Patricios* under Cariaga and by the Galicians and Andalucians. Another unit of the *Patricios* was situated in front of the Cabildo and in the Calle de las Torres. Four more companies of the regiment, under Saavedra, defended the college of San Carlos and others the neighbouring houses further south towards the Fortress. The artillery of the Cantabros and the Montaneses was positioned near the Santa Domingo church and the Catalonians were used as riflemen in various parts of the city. The remainder of Liniers' force was held in reserve in the main plazas and at the Fortress where his headquarters was established. The isolated post of the Retiro was placed under the command of De la Concha with the marines, two companies of *Patricios*, under Pereira and Alvarez, and one company of Galicians under Varela. This then was the position of Liniers' force of 3 July.

Whitelocke's army, with the exception of Mahon's detachment, had united on the west side of the city and were now together for the first time since the landing at Ensenada on 28 June. Earlier on 3 July Whitelocke had ordered Gower to summon the city to surrender and accordingly Major Roache, with one officer, twelve riflemen and two Spanish prisoners as guides, set off into the city under a flag of truce. 'I penetrated a considerable way into the town.' recalled Roache,

> The houses were all barricaded and shut up, and the town appeared to be in great confusion; all description of people, men and boys were armed, paying very little respect to the flag of truce and but for the rifle corps I am sure I could not have got back. I was stopped less than a quarter of a mile from the Fort, and with great difficulty I approached an officer and asked to be introduced to the Spanish authority. After an hour and a half General Elio with other officers came to me and said I could not see General Liniers on any account. I told him I had the honour to carry proposals for the surrender of the town. General Elio conversed with great animation and, pressing his hand upon his breast, he said, they possessed sufficient strength and

spirit to defend the town, that I should return to my general in order that he might make communication as he thought proper in writing. He never let me enter into the particulars of my instructions, though I endeavoured to represent to them our force and impress upon their mind the effusion of blood that must follow further hostilities.[18]

Roache returned to Gower and told him what had happened. Gower then wrote another letter which Roache again carried back to the same spot. Elio had gone but the message was given to an aide-de-camp. The letter set out certain conditions of surrender, namely, that all military and civil officers would be made prisoners of war, that all British prisoners in possession of the Spaniards would be returned, that a free exercise of the Roman Catholic religion would be granted and that all property would be respected provided the owner took an oath of fidelity to the British government. Once again Elio gave the reply and again it was predictable. He said he would not entertain any suggestions of surrender and added that there were more than enough troops ready to defend the city. Roache again returned to Gower with his summons rejected.

By now the whole British army was drawn up at the Corrale del Miserere. The outposts had been engaged by small parties of the enemy but nothing serious happened. The rain soon began to fall heavily and the men took shelter in houses for the night which gave them a chance to consume their rations of bread and spirit and also to get some well earned rest. That night Whitelocke asked Gower whether he had formulated any plan of attack as the latter had been in the suburbs for twenty-four hours. As one historian later wrote:

> Gower, who from the start to finish appears to have been the evil genius of the campaign, at once produced a cut and dried scheme, probably one of the most curious and unpractical which ever emanated from the brain of a general officer.[19]

On paper the plan seemed simple enough. The army would enter the city along all but the four central streets as far as the river, so as to be able to attack the Plaza Mayor from both flanks. The army would be split into thirteen different columns, one of which would take the Plaza de Toros, a key position at the north-eastern angle of the city, whilst the other columns were to push on to the river taking other key points. They would then form up on the roofs from where they would be able to command the city and then dictate terms to the Spaniards. Whitelocke at once decided to adopt the plan and the next morning, the 4th, he summoned to his headquarters, which he had established at the house of the American, White, those officers who would have to lead the columns into the streets of Buenos Aires.

The plan was unveiled and following the briefing Whitelocke announced, much to his officers' surprise, his intention to begin the attack at noon that very day. Auchmuty, however, argued against this, pointing out the fact that none of the officers had any knowledge at all of the ground over which they would have to attack and would need time to prepare. He also queried the wisdom of attacking a large city in broad daylight. Gower surprisingly supported these arguments and the attack was put back until dawn the next morning.

It is strange to relate that none of the British officers raised any objections to Gower's plan, not even Pack who, in the light of his experiences during Beresford's invasion, knew Buenos Aires better than anyone. At Whitelocke's trial, however, he did say that in his opinion the commander-in-chief seemed to be acting against his better judgement. The failings of Gower's plan must have seemed obvious to Craufurd also, especially when we recall the conversation he had with Whitelocke in Montevideo when the latter pointed out the dangers of exposing the British troops to an attack upon a city such as Montevideo or Buenos Aires where the flat roofs and well built parapets would give excellent cover to the defenders without them having to expose themselves to any real danger. Craufurd, however, said nothing.

The plan had been decided upon but even at this late stage Whitelocke still hoped he might be able to avoid the bloodshed which would inevitably follow the storming of the city and he decided to send another message to Liniers, summoning him to surrender. This time it was carried by Captain Samuel Whittingham who, with a strong detachment, rode towards the centre of the city under a flag of truce to ask for a parley with Liniers. The Spanish commander sent Hilarion de la Quintana to meet him but the people, seeing the British officer, suspected treachery and began firing on the escort which was forced back leaving fourteen men behind them. Eventually Quintana reached Whittingham and conducted him to Liniers who duly read the summons before writing his reply:

> I have just received Your Excellency's despatch of today's date, and have the honour to inform you that whilst I have administration and the present spirit of the garrison and the inhabitants continues to exist, I will never admit any proposition for the surrender of the place that has been entrusted to my charge as I am confident that I have sufficient means to resist every opposition. Your Excellency may bring upon me. The rights of humanity to which Your Excellency refers, no matter what the result of combat, have been violated more by you as aggressor than by me, who does no more than comply with my duty and the just cause of reprisal.[20]

This reply convinced Whitelocke that an assault was now inevitable and he determined to carry out his plan to attack the city at dawn the next day.

The city of Buenos Aires has already been described but nevertheless let us look again before dealing with the actual assault.

The city was laid out in rectangular blocks, each one about a hundred and thirty yards square, with the city's eastern face bordering on the Rio de la Plata. The city itself was about two miles long from north to south and one mile wide from east to west. The ground sloped gently down from the Corrale del Miserere, which overlooked the whole city, to the river. The Fortress was built close to the shore in the middle of the eastern edge of the city. Its walls were fifteen feet high but apart from the wall facing the city there was no ditch around them. There were several high buildings around it which, if occupied, were capable of dominating the place, so that it was not of any great strategic importance. Its west wall faced out onto the Plaza Mayor, the scene of Beresford's unsuccessful defence the year before. This was divided by an arcade called the Recova. To the north-west of the plaza stood the Cathedral and about a mile further north was the important post of the Plaza de Toros, the bull-ring, with the artillery barracks and the arsenal beyond it. South of the Plaza Mayor, four blocks away, was the convent of Santa Domingo, the second largest church in Buenos Aires. Further south was the Residencia, a large building standing within a quadrilateral, one third of which was open and the rest occupied by buildings. The Residencia was a key position as it was not dominated by any other building which meant that if the British could take it, along with the Fortress and the Plaza de Toros, they would have almost total control of the city. This then was Buenos Aires.

The British troops who were to make the assault were drawn up in a line, running north to south, six hundred yards to the east of the Corrale del Miserere, facing the city at a distance of about three miles from the Fortress. They numbered about 5,650 including a reserve of 1,100 which was to be held back at White's house, and a further 600 who were also to be held ready to act in support of the other storming columns. Whitelocke's orders for the assault were as follows:

> The 38th Regiment, under Sir Samuel Auchmuty, to detach and possess itself of the Plaza de Toros, and the adjacent strong ground, and then take post. The 5th, 36th, 87th and 88th Regiments to be divided into wings, and each wing to penetrate into the street directly in its front.
>
> The eight battalions divided into wings each followed by a wing of the 95th Regiment, and a 3-pounder to proceed down the two streets in the right of the central one, and the 45th Regiment down the two adjoining; and after clearing the streets of the enemy to take post at the Residencia.
>
> Two 6-pounders covered by the carbineers and the three troops of the 9th Light Dragoons, to proceed along the central street. The remainder of the carbineers and the dragoons to act as a reserve in the centre.
>
> Each division to proceed along the street directly in its front, till it arrives at the last square of houses next the Rio de la Plata, of which it is to possess

itself forming on the flat roofs and there wait for further orders. The 95th Regiment to occupy two of the most commanding situations from which it can annoy the enemy.

Two corporals, with tools, to march at the head of each column, for the purpose of breaking open the doors.

The whole to be unloaded, and no firing to be permitted until the columns reach their final points and form.

A cannonade in the centre to be the signal for the whole to move forward.

The most controversial clause here was the last but one, which stated that the men were to enter the city unloaded. It was said that this was to prevent the danger to the head of the column which would be increased by the firing from the back of the column. It was this clause that would later cause a storm of controversy, particularly at Whitelocke's trial.

The night of 4 July arrived with the British soldiers resting, the night before a battle always being a time for thought, whilst the inhabitants and soldiers in Buenos Aires passed the night preparing for the assault which they now knew would come the next day.

VII

La Defensa

The morning of 5 July 1807, dawned overcast, hazy and gloomy, a typical winter's day in Buenos Aires. The British troops destined to attack the city formed before daybreak with the head of each column facing down the street along which it was to advance. Orders had been given which stated that the columns were not to go beyond the British advance posts until the signal for the commencement of the attack, which was to be the firing of a single cannon. The gun was fired promptly at half past-six and slowly the columns began to move forward in the gloomy stillness to begin the assault, the silence soon to be shattered by the sounds of bugles, drums, muskets, cannons and the shouts of the population as the city rose to meet them.

In order to tell the story of what happened that day in July it is necessary to follow each of the columns individually, beginning with that under Sir Samuel Auchmuty.

LA DEFENSA: THE LEFT WING

Auchmuty's brigade started on the north or far left of the British line, and on the firing of the signal it began to march east through the darkness along the deserted streets of Buenos Aires. The column marched in sections formed by seven men in rank by seven in file and entered the streets in double time. All was quiet, save for the shuffling of the troops' feet, and not a soul was to be seen, not that it was possible to see any great distance anyway, given the gloom of the early morning.

The column had gone about a mile and had met virtually no resistance at all when suddenly the British troops were hit by a tremendous fire of grape-shot from two guns placed directly in front of them. In the narrow confines of the street the effect of this fire was, of course, devastating, particularly on the grenadiers at the front of the column. But the men pushed on until they came under a heavy fire of musketry from the Spanish defenders in the Plaza de Toros, a twelve-sided building which from the outside looked like a blank wall with a gallery above from which the Spanish sharpshooters could fire without danger to themselves. This bull-ring was defended by about a thousand men of the Galician Regiment under the command of Guitierrez de la Concha and Jacob Varela and their guns raked the British column which, being totally exposed, began to waver and slowly come to a halt before seeking shelter from the heavy enemy fire.

The right wing of the 87th Regiment was commanded by Sir Edward Butler who ordered the men to break into a garden on their right which they succeeded in doing and through this they found themselves in a street running parallel to the one from which they had just fled. Here they found a deep watercourse running down the street which gave them shelter from the enemy's musketry and cannon. This watercourse led down to the river. Here, Auchmuty and Butler gathered their men together in and around a large house they had occupied. They had suffered quite serious losses from the fire of the defenders in the Plaza de Toros and also from those who had sprung up on the rooftops of nearly every house to pour a heavy fire into the advancing column.

As he took stock of the situation Auchmuty was joined by the left wing of the 87th under Major Miller, whose men had also been heavily engaged. Miller's men, however, had been slightly more successful and had killed and wounded a large number of the enemy and had taken about a hundred prisoners as well as three field pieces. During his attack Miller said he had seen the colours of the 5th Regiment flying above the convent of St. Catalina. This came as welcome news as it meant that his right flank was secure. Thus, he was now able to send parties to clear out some enemy soldiers who had been firing down on him from a house in his rear. Following this Miller continued until he finally joined up with Auchmuty and Butler. Having been checked by the heavy enemy fire from the Plaza de Toros and from the rooftops around him, Auchmuty halted with both wings of the 87th to await further developments.

On the right of Auchmuty's brigade the 5th Regiment had advanced into the city where the right wing of the regiment made good progress without any trouble at all. The troops marched quickly but warily along the gloomy streets but met with no opposition and soon reached the banks of the river where the men raised the King's Colour upon the tower of the convent of St. Catalina. Inside the convent were the nuns of the Dominican Order who found themselves caught between the fire of the Spanish defenders of both the Fortress and the Retiro. The Mother Prioress later recalled the moment when the 5th, under Colonel Humphrey Davie, burst into the church:

We were terrified as the hatchets tore down the outer portals of the convent amidst the shouts of the soldiers and at the tremendous blows at the locks of the chapel, the only wall that still defended us.[1]

When the British troops burst into the chapel they found the Mother Prioress holding aloft the sacred chalice whilst about seventy nuns gathered round her, the long white veils of their order covering their faces. The nuns received the troops kneeling in silence and each one of them had prepared with Holy Communion to meet their deaths which they thought they were about to receive, especially as the British had burst in with fixed bayonets, their muskets pointing straight at the nuns. Not one of the nuns moved or broke the silence.

Death was that which we feared least, considering it to be the will of God that we should make the sacrifice for the triumph of our cause. To our immense surprise this legion of wolves accustomed to the deeds of horror accompanying warfare, displayed utmost respect for our religious calling, never offending us in anyway and slowly disappearing into the convent. The dreariness of the day and the sadness of the circumstances rendered the obscurity of the chapel more intense, and we were unable to distinguish whether it was morning, noon or night. We remained in the chapel until six in the evening of the following day, fasting with no other sustenance than that derived from the Sacred Host, received the day before, to give us strength.[2]

The nuns were thus spared and the British troops disappeared into the convent to take up positions from where they could carry on the attack.

The left wing of the 5th Regiment was under the command of Major Henry King and it had not gone very far into the city before it ran into a storm of musketry from the Spanish defenders. King's column rushed forward, the leading section with fixed bayonets. As they ran down the street four pieces of cannon were abandoned to them by the enemy, they having shot the horses first. The column rushed on without stopping until it reached the river. Here, King halted and looked around for the most eligible houses in which to establish himself. Whilst he was doing this a heavy firing was heard on his left and soon afterwards Major Miller and Captain Rose, of the 87th, came up the street and told him that their regiment had been halted with heavy loss, and on hearing this King decided to stay where he was and set up headquarters. King's men duly broke into a house and raised the regimental colour of the 5th above it. No sooner had they done so, however, than the enemy opened fire on the house with a blaze of musketry from some rooftops to their right. King immediately detached Captains Clark and Drury with their companies to occupy a church a short distance away and also to break into some other houses with the intention of keeping down the fire of the Spaniards.

The firing on King's position increased steadily, and one man was killed and two wounded on top of the roof as they stood with him. As casualties mounted the lower part of the house was occupied by the wounded who were treated by Assistant-Surgeon Bone. Bayonet parties eventually cleared the neighbouring houses, the enemy units being scattered, for the time being at least. The firing continued on King's position, however, from the Plaza de Toros but this was at long range and he managed to hold on to his position until at about nine o'clock that morning when the firing stopped. This was mainly due to the attack by the 38th Regiment under Colonel Nugent.

Nugent's column had set off at half-past six at the start of the attack and twenty minutes later found itself in a narrow lane leading to the Plaza de Toros. At the end of this lane was a large house which was occupied by the enemy who kept up a sharp fire on Nugent's men as they approached. This house was called the house of Azcuenaga and after a determined effort the 38th forced the door and rushed in, bayoneting all the defenders inside. This still left the Plaza de Toros, however, which was defended by several guns and it was obvious that unless this could be taken the attack in this part of the city would fail. Nugent's men suffered several casualties trying to take it. As well as the guns inside, the Spaniards also had numerous pieces on the outside which Nugent tried to take. But each time his men approached they were met by a galling fire from all directions and eventually he gave up the attempt, having lost many men. Instead, he determined to take a large house by the river which was occupied by the enemy. By doing this he hoped to silence the Spanish guns outside the Plaza de Toros and then turn the enemy's right flank.

On having decided to take the house a party of the 38th stormed forward and threw themselves against the door, forcing it open, whereupon a single grenadier, said to have been one of the worst characters in the regiment, dashed in and rushed to the roof where he came across fifteen enemy soldiers. He bayoneted two of them whilst the rest pretended to be dead in the hope that they might be spared by this fearsome, enraged British soldier. Suddenly, four other Spaniards came at him but he bayoneted one of them and was about to deal with the others when his comrades arrived and every one of the defenders was quickly put to the sword. The 38th soon took possession of another house and from its roof opened up a heavy fire on the gunners in front of the Plaza de Toros. This was too much for them to bear and apart from a single battery that remained firing they spiked their guns and retreated to the safety of the building itself. The battery that remained was quickly dealt with when a group of the 38th charged from the back of a house and fell upon the gunners, about sixty in all, and chased them into a barracks where, after some savage hand-to-hand fighting, the British troops put every single gunner to death. Fortunately for the British the Spaniards had left one of their guns unspiked and this was quickly turned around and used against the Plaza de Toros.

Shortly after this the 38th were joined by Auchmuty and the 87th Regiment. When he arrived Auchmuty found Colonel Nugent in possession of the Spanish artillery, all of their stores and a few buildings, but he had yet to take the bull-ring itself. Nugent's men, however, were setting about the place with a 12-pounder that had been brought up to fire at close range from the shelter of a house whilst other units of the 38th were busy keeping down the fire of the defenders from the other side of the bull-ring. As soon as they arrived the 87th took possession of the houses and rooftops surrounding the Plaza de Toros and proceeded to open up a galling fire on the defenders inside who were quickly running out of ammunition.

In fact, an ammunition park lay not more than a hundred yards away but De la Concha, in command, made no attempt to reach it. Jacob Varela, of the Galicians, urged De la Concha to abandon the post and retreat to the main body of the army elsewhere in the city but he would not move. Therefore, it was left to Varela and just sixty of his men to make good their escape, the party arriving safely behind the convent of Santa Domingo where they took up a position in part of the southern line of defence. The British troops then stepped up their efforts to take the Plaza de Toros and soon it became impossible for the defenders to hold on any longer. It was too late for De la Concha and the remaining defenders to retreat, however, and at about nine o'clock that morning the white flag was raised and all of them were made prisoners, nearly a thousand in all with thirty-two guns.

With the Plaza de Toros in British hands Major King, with the 5th Regiment, tried to advance once more but again had not gone far before his men came under fire from the defenders on the rooftops around them. Again they were forced to break into some houses. Here, they entered a courtyard where the men formed up and made another charge down the street but the opposition was too much. Losses were heavy and King's men were forced back to the house where the wounded were brought in and treated. At this point King sent Captain Phillips to go to the church where Lieutenant-Colonel Davie was in order to ask for reinforcements.

Meanwhile, King's men, in a mood of grim determination, urged him to make another attack on a house where an enemy flag was seen flying. They charged and tried to break in but the heavy door would not give. As they struggled to smash it down casualties mounted, and with men dropping at every enemy discharge King was once again forced to abandon the attack and return to the courtyard. In this latest attack King himself was wounded in the head by a spent ball and was also slightly wounded in the arm. By now, the Spaniards had brought up two guns which began to sweep the streets with grapeshot. In such closed-in conditions grapeshot was devastating and it would take a brave man to lead his troops against such lethal opposition. However, King knew that parties of the enemy were attempting to surround him and cut him off and knew he must move soon or risk being taken. But just as he was about to withdraw he received a message from General Lumley ordering not to retreat on any account because he covered the latter's flank. King knew he must disobey this, however, as he preferred to carry out the retreat and fight on rather than risk the certain destruction of his column.

As his men prepared to run the gauntlet of the Spanish guns Captain Ridge came to King and informed him that a party of the enemy were advancing up the street and that the men wanted permission to charge them. Ridge, later to die heroically during the Peninsular War as the first man inside the fortress of Badajoz, was bleeding from a leg wound but he formed up the men of the 5th who advanced along the street to meet the enemy. The guns had stopped, the Spaniards not wanting to hit their own men, and the British troops extended across the street, the leading section at the charge. They had gone only a short way, however, when a dense mass of cavalry dressed in yellow jackets came around the corner at a gentle trot. All, at once a shout went up, 'they mean to surrender!' and sure enough one of the horsemen was carrying a white flag. As King's men approached, the Spaniards began to wave their hands making signals not to fire and an officer came forward with a white handkerchief. King naturally assumed the Spaniards wished to surrender and he halted his men who formed across the street. The officer advanced and King went to meet him, telling him he was a prisoner. The Spaniard seemed to understand and shook hands with King who saw that the rest of the Spaniards were following close behind, some with swords in their hands and some with pistols. Both King and Ridge made signs to them to lay down their arms but as they refused to do so King boldly grabbed two or three of them and threw their weapons to the ground. At this moment one of them presented his pistol at King which the latter parried with his sword. One of King's men then rushed forward at the Spaniard with his bayonet but the Spaniard jumped aside at the last moment and it only tore his clothes.

By now King was having difficulty restraining his men who suspected treachery from the Spaniards who were growing in number every minute and who were drawn up in thick ranks across the street, ready to charge. Before them stood King, sword in hand, with just five companies of the 5th. King suspected treachery but his men still thought the enemy wished to surrender. Then, suddenly, and to their amazement, the Spaniards insisted that the British themselves surrender and the officer demanded King's sword. At this point the fearless Briton, without flinching, calmly raised his sword and held it at the Spaniard's breast, demanding his own sword, at which the officer unbuckled it and gave it to him. The Spaniard was then taken prisoner. Just as he was being marched away, however, there was a shout from Ensign Harvey, who carried the regimental colour, that the Spaniards were trying to seize it whilst at the same time some of the Spanish cavalry picked up their arms. By now King had had enough of the Spaniards' tricks and gave the order to charge, at which, 'the scoundrels immediately turned and ran, and galloped off as fast as possible, turning down the first streets they came to,' followed by a volley from the 5th. The Spaniards left behind them twelve dead, and from accounts left to us by various British officers it seems as though it was a common ploy throughout the day for the Spaniards to advance under the protection of a white flag, their real intention being to lure the British troops into a trap.

Stephen Morley, a sergeant with the 5th, said that at this point they could see a British flag waving proudly above a sort of turret. This, together with the fact that they had just repelled the Spanish cavalry, as well as having cleared every street, made a number of prisoners, and had beaten off every attack, led him and his comrades to believe that victory was at hand. There were, however, one or two signs that made him rather uneasy. He had noticed, as had his comrades, that the firing which had earlier been heavy in the different parts of the city had slackened. Yet no part of the army, nor of the other wing of the 5th, under Davie, had joined them.

In spite of this, King assembled his men and proposed an attack on the Plaza Mayor which was heavily defended by the enemy. But with spirits high all the officers and men were behind him. Morley relates that there was a sergeant with them, George Golland, who he believed would have gladly sabred the first man who showed symptoms of what he never felt, namely fear.

With the regimental colour in front of them, King and the men of the 5th set off down a street leading to the Plaza Mayor but their bold effort was in vain. They had not gone far before they came under a galling fire from the defenders and were forced back with some loss. On their way back King found the rest of the regiment under Davie as well as some stragglers from other units. At this point came the first hint of failure and the first criticism of Whitelocke:

> After this failure, victory was out of the question; we had no leader to animate us, no orders, no official authority; our exertions ceased. We marched to the bull-ring where our colours were still flying.[3]

When King and Davie reached the Plaza de Toros with the 5th they found Auchmuty with the 87th and 38th Regiments still waiting there. Everyone was tired and somewhat depleted after the morning's fighting and all three regiments could do no more than take up positions there and wait.

LA DEFENSA: THE ATTACK IN THE CENTRE

In all, the British attack on the left of their line had gone relatively well. In spite of their heavy casualties, they had taken the Plaza de Toros, the most commanding point in the city, and had captured over a thousand prisoners along with thirty-two guns. Elsewhere, however, the attack had not gone so well.

To the immediate south of Auchmuty's brigade, Lumley had met with almost total disaster. Lumley himself commanded the right wing of the 36th Regiment and had entered Buenos Aires by the Calles San Nicolas and Parque. The regiment had left its packs and greatcoats in camp but progress was still slow owing to the bad state of the road along which the troops advanced. Soon after entering the first street Lumley's men were given a taste of what to expect later, for the gloom of early dawn was lit up here and there by flashes of musketry that blazed away at them from all directions.

In spite of this the column reached a street adjoining the river but the men found that the pick-axes issued to them were practically useless in breaking open the strong doors and windows of the houses and it was only at some length that they managed to break into a few houses near the river. Here there was a small beach and Lumley occupied a large house that backed onto it and established his headquarters there whilst the colours of the 36th were hoisted onto the roof of the house as a signal and to encourage the other columns of his brigade. No sooner had the colours been unfurled, however, than the Spanish troops in the Fortress and in part of the Plaza Mayor opened up on them with seven guns that began to sweep the streets with showers of grape shot. A heavy fire also opened up on them from what seemed to Lumley like every direction. Again, the British troops were unable to detect the Spanish marksmen, hidden as they were behind the parapets of the houses.

Lumley's men had been by the beach and in the houses nearby for a short while when they saw a group of red-coated soldiers running towards them. These turned out to be Lieutenant-Colonel Robert Burne with a party of the 36th Regiment who had earlier spiked two enemy guns near the Fortress. No sooner had they accomplished this than they themselves came under fire from all around them. For some time they remained under cover at the back of some houses before receiving orders to join the rest of the regiment whose position Burne could see along the beach. Another group of the 36th were making their way through the streets with a large number of prisoners they had taken. The prisoners, like the British troops, invariably came under fire from their own people, particularly at one point from two guns in front of them. One British officer, seeing this, pushed the prisoners round the corner of another street in an attempt to get them out of the firing line. But scarcely had he done so than the Spanish gunners, on seeing that there was no longer any danger of hitting their own people, opened fire with grape shot. The effect in the confined space was devastating. Every man of the leading section, save one, was killed and the captain of the company knocked down with his breastplate forced into his breast, his sword broken in two and his clothes torn to ribbons. The rest of the party escaped and reached the main body of the regiment on the beach whilst the wounded officer was spared, the enemy not thinking it worthwhile to fire on a single man. He too reached the regiment's colours.

The regiment now found itself in a perilous position. On each of its flanks were parallel streets defended by 24-pounders and strong bodies of enemy troops who were killing or wounding almost every man that appeared at the corners of the streets. 'To retreat was impossible; to advance, certain destruction.'[4] Faced with such a situation, therefore, Lumley and the 36th had no other choice than to remain by the beach and hold their position.

The 88th Regiment, meanwhile, had gone into action on Lumley's right and it too had met with stiff opposition. In fact, it would not be too much to say that the regiment had met with total disaster. The right wing of the 88th was under the command of Major Vandeleur, and it had gone a short way down the street when an enemy vidette appeared. As the British troops advanced the Spaniards retreated down the street, occasionally looking up and speaking to the people on top of the houses. When Vandeleur had got about a third of the way down the street these people suddenly opened up a heavy fire on his men from behind the parapets of the houses and from the windows above him. Immediately, the British troops were ordered to advance in double quick time which they did, cheering as they went.

As they charged up the street they were assailed from both sides of it with 'muskets, hand-grenades, stink-pots, brick-bats, and all sorts of combustibles.' These stink-pots were probably some sort of incendiary device which gave off much smoke and fire when exploded. The column struggled on through a storm of lead until it eventually arrived at a breastwork made of hides filled with earth which was thrown up across the street. The men scrambled breathlessly over it and found themselves in a ditch, six feet deep and some twelve feet wide. They quickly evacuated this spot as they found themselves easy prey for the Spanish guns in the Plaza Mayor. On leaving the ditch Vandeleur and his men charged down a street leading to the river but this was enfiladed by the guns in the Fortress and again they were forced back, the party taking shelter in a house after forcing the door with the butts of their muskets. Vandeleur tried to place some of his men on the roof but the enemy had it covered and any man who showed himself on top came under fire. Soon afterwards the Spaniards brought up a field piece against Vandeleur. However, in a ditch nearby was Captain

Chisholm with a party of men who opened up on the enemy gunners, forcing them to abandon it. Chisholm's men themselves now became pinned down by the enemy marksmen on the rooftops and soon the 88th found itself in a desperate situation.

Vandeleur was completely surrounded, half of his men were either dead or wounded and there was no hope of retreating or receiving any support as the sounds of battle elsewhere in the city began to move farther away from him, indicating to him that something had gone wrong with the attack around him. He had occupied some houses in the hope of hanging on until help could be got to him but the enemy succeeded in knocking down the backs of two of the houses which meant that all the British wounded had to be moved into one house along with those still fighting. Shot and shell flew all around them as the Spaniards pounded away at the houses. Conditions inside grew steadily worse until at about eleven o'clock that morning Vandeleur called his officers together. There was no sign of any other British units and the only firing they could hear was that which was directed against them. It was obvious to him and his officers that with so many wounded men lying around in need of attention that it was impossible to carry on the attack and they decided to hoist a white flag. Immediately a Spanish officer jumped up from behind a wall and asked upon what terms Vandeleur wished to surrender. He replied that he only asked quarter and care of the wounded. The Spanish officer put his hand on his breast and said that they were Spaniards and as such always treated their prisoners well. Upon this Vandeleur surrendered his sword following which the officer gave a shout and from behind walls and other concealed places there arose an immense number of the enemy who jumped onto the tops of the houses around the 88th's position as well as that in which they were held up. The Spaniards took the arms from the British troops who were then led away to various prisons in the city whilst the officers were conducted to the Fortress.

The other wing of the 88th Regiment, under Lieutenant-Colonel Alexander Duff, met with a similar fate. To start with, this wing had been considered so weak by Duff that he sent a request to headquarters to ask for two more companies. When these two arrived, however, Duff received a shock. To his amazement the troops sent to him arrived without flints in their muskets. He asked Major Ironmonger, who was with them, for an explanation. He replied by saying that General Gower had directed him to take the flints out at which Duff ordered the major to get new ones from other companies if any could be spared. Not all of the troops got them, however, and some of those who did were later reported to have been shot dead whilst in the act of putting them in their muskets.

The order to attack with muskets unloaded or without flints was later put on the charge sheet at Whitelocke's court martial. It was one of the more controversial aspects of the day's fighting yet one can possible forgive him for ordering the columns to advance unloaded so as not to endanger those at the front of the column. Also, it is interesting to note that of the charges against him Whitelocke was acquitted of only one, namely that which related to him having ordered the attack to take place with muskets unloaded. However, to the British soldiers now attacking the hostile city of Buenos Aires the order seemed like madness. In fact, so pessimistic was Duff as to the outcome of the attack that he ordered the colours to be left behind at headquarters in case they were taken by the enemy. His fears, unfortunately, were well founded.

The attack got off to a reasonably good start with his men reaching the church of La Merced without a shot being fired in opposition. When they entered the gateway, however, the situation changed drastically, for no sooner had Duff's men set foot inside than the enemy opened up a tremendous fire on them from the houses opposite. Soon, nearly thirty men lay in the gateway and finding it impossible to break into the church itself with the pick-axes given to him he decided to leave the position and struggle on further into the city in the hope of gaining a more advantageous position. Duff set off towards the Fortress with a heavy fire of musketry following him and his men through the streets. He had lost between eighty and a hundred men killed and wounded and was forced to seek cover in three houses.

Duff formed his men on the roofs of two of these houses and engaged the enemy in a fire fight. He held his position for four hours, losing men all the time in a desperate struggle against a seemingly invisible enemy. The Spaniards had Duff surrounded and like Vandeleur with the other wing of the 88th he soon noticed that the fighting in other parts of the city had died away. He too called together those officers still on their feet and asked for their opinions. Again, with no support forthcoming and with the casualties building up around them the opinion was that they should surrender. Therefore, at a quarter to twelve in the morning Duff's wing of the 88th Regiment surrendered and the men were marched off to the Fortress as prisoners, surrounded as they went by about three or four thousand of the enemy. When they arrived at the Fortress they found Vandeleur who had surrendered earlier. It was then that their fears as to the outcome of the attack began to come true. Duff had lost seventeen officers and 220 men killed and wounded in the attack which had gone as badly as he had feared. Only a handful of his men managed to escape, scrambling over the rooftops to rejoin Lumley and inform him of the disaster; Lumley already knew, however, for the Spaniards were now throwing all of their men in that part of the city against him.

We last saw Lumley pinned down on the beach awaiting support but none was forthcoming and at two o'clock in the afternoon he collected his men together and began making his way towards Auchmuty at the Plaza de Toros, all the way under fire from all around him. Eventually he rejoined Auchmuty at around three o'clock having suffered heavy casualties and having gained absolutely nothing in return. Such were the fortunes of the British attacks by Auchmuty and Lumley on the left and in the Centre of Buenos Aires. It now only remains to follow the fortunes of the attack by the right of the British army to the south of the city.

LA DEFENSA: THE RIGHT OF THE LINE

The attack by the right of the British line began with the 45th Regiment, which advanced in two wings, the left under Major Nicholls and the right under Lieutenant-Colonel Guard. The regiment was to occupy the Residencia, at the south-eastern angle of the city, and at daybreak the two columns moved off, marching down separate streets for about three quarters of a mile until they met up at a junction. The 45th soon reached the Residencia which was quickly and easily occupied with the loss of only three men killed. As the British troops forced the entrance a white flag was held over a wall by a friar who had unfortunately been wounded. Two companies were placed inside, four more took up positions in some adjacent houses and another company was sent to clear away parties of enemy sharpshooters. The occupation of the Residencia meant that not only had the British gained possession of a strong and vital position secur-ing their flank but they also had direct communication with the fleet still moored in the river.

To the left of the 45th the Light Brigade had gone into action, also in two wings. The right wing consisted of four companies of the 95th Rifles and four light companies under Craufurd. The left wing consisted of four more companies of the 95th and five companies of light infantry, commanded by Denis Pack. Pack's column was quickly engaged in heavy fighting and once again the men were not helped by Whitelocke's order forbidding the men to march with flints in their muskets:

> We remained under arms on the 5th of July, waiting the order to advance. Judge our astonishment when the word was given to march without ammunition, with fixed bayonets only. 'We are betrayed!' was whispered through the ranks. 'Mind your duty, my lads; onwards, onwards, Britain for ever!' were the last words I heard our noble Captain Brookman utter. He fell as we entered the town.[5]

For the first few yards Pack's men advanced almost unnoticed. Indeed, Pack was struck by the extraordinary stillness of the place which was bro-ken only by a few random shots now and then, mainly at extreme range from the Plaza Mayor. The real opposition began when he came in sight of the river. Here, the resistance became markedly stronger with the main

Spanish position being situated in the Plaza. There were marksmen concealed in every house, at the windows and on the roofs and these opened a heavy fire on Pack's tightly packed column which was unable to return the fire. The British troops rushed on carrying everything before them, scrambling over ditches and other obstacles that were placed in their path by the inhabitants of the city. At the corner of every street, and flanking all the ditches, they had placed guns that thinned the British ranks with every discharge.

During the attack many British troops stopped to plunder the houses, making sallies to bring out articles they could not possibly use or get away. But plunder has always been a great temptation, one which many a soldier has been unable to resist. It was one which often led to their death. Indeed, one sergeant of the 38th had made a hole in his canteen into which he slipped all the money he could lay his hands on, but as he came out of one house he was shot through the head and in his fall the canteen burst and a large number of coins ran about in all directions in the street. There commenced a great scramble for the money and about eighteen men were likewise shot, grasping for the money they were never to enjoy. They snatched it from their dying companions, although they themselves were to be in the same situation the next moment.

Pack's column managed to find some shelter and as the firing momentarily died down he decided to divide his command into two. Colonel Cadogan would take command of the other half of the column to attack the Jesuit College, inside the grounds of which was situated the barracks of the regiment of *Patricios*. Cadogan's men marched warily along the street in silence. By now the day was fully broken and the lamps which had been burning all night were beginning to flicker out. To the north the sound of gunfire could be heard as the other British columns attacked. As he approached the college Cadogan halted his column in order to bring up a small 3-pounder with which he intended to blow open the gate. Suddenly, a Spanish voice was heard, giving the order to fire. All hell broke loose as the *Patricios*, under their commander, Saavedra, appeared on the roofs and in the windows of the houses on both sides of the street to unleash a devastating fire of musketry into the British column which reeled back, every man of the leading company being shot down in an instant. It was impossible for Cadogan to take the college and equally impossible to penetrate any further up the street. He was therefore obliged to fall back and throw himself, along with about 140 of his men, into a house about 150 yards from the college. The remainder of his unit dispersed into several houses adjoining and those who were unable to do so were either killed or wounded.

Pack's own column had met with a similar fate and he himself later said that he was convinced he had entered upon 'a contest the most unequal, perhaps, that was ever fought.' His men suffered severely at the hands of a seemingly invisible enemy. He himself was wounded, and had been forced to retreat along the very street along which he had originally advanced. Here he met Cadogan, at the house inside which the latter had taken shelter from the fire of the *Patricios*. Pack told Cadogan to abandon the house and withdraw with him to the relative safety of the Residencia and added that he thought Cadogan to be in an impossible position. The latter, however, refused to give up a place which he said had been gained at such a heavy price and he remained inside with his men whilst Pack continued his withdrawal. The house in which Cadogan and his men were grimly holding out was the house of the Vicereina, the wife of the Viceroy, and here took place one of the most famous and bloodiest episodes of the day's fighting.

The house had been quickly surrounded by the Spaniards and a tremendous fire fight developed between the British troops on the roof and the Spanish troops on top of the surrounding buildings. The British had some measure of cover on the roof but it was not adequate enough to protect them from the hail of shot that was turned against them by the Spaniards. Such was the ferocity of the fight that it was said the drainpipes flowed with the blood of the dead, dying and wounded British soldiers. They defended the post as long as they could but it soon became obvious that, as no help was forthcoming and with such heavy odds against them, they were fighting a losing battle. The post had been defended for nearly three hours with the loss of one sergeant and fourteen men killed, and five officers and eighty-two men wounded. The carnage on the roof was appalling but in spite of it the British troops thought they were giving as good as they were receiving.

This seemed to be confirmed when during a brief lull a Spanish officer appeared over a wall with a flag of truce. Cadogan thought this could only mean that the Spaniards wanted to surrender and after a consultation with his officers agreed to a parley. All firing ceased from the top of the house upon which the enemy poured over the rooftops in great numbers, it having really been the intention of the Spanish officer to summon Cadogan to surrender. The British commander was thus left only to look around at the pitifully small group of soldiers still on their feet with him to realise that further resistance would be useless. After a word with his brother officers Cadogan and his men surrendered.

Pack, meanwhile, had managed to find Craufurd's column at the convent of Santa Domingo, where he had been joined by Guard with some of the 45th Regiment. Craufurd, still seething at the lost opportunity following the fight at the Corrale, had formed his brigade earlier that morning and had advanced into the city along the two roads allotted to them according to Gower's plan.

The enemy, as it had been reported at headquarters on the 4th, had concentrated their principal force in a position forming a square, having within it the market place, and the Fort in the middle of its eastern face; and as we entered the town on the right of this position, the left column of my brigade under Lieutenant-Colonel Pack, was of course the nearest to the south face of the enemy's position, and came first into action. I with the right column passed quite through the town, and arrived with the head of it on the beach, without meeting any obstacle or seeing anything but small straggling parties of the enemy. When I arrived on the beach I saw the south-eastern bastion of the Fort at a distance of about 450 yards from me, as nearly as I can judge; and being of the opinion that by remaining where I then was, I should not have fulfilled the object of the disposition, I determined to advance upon the Fort.[6]

So ran Craufurd's account of the beginning of his adventures in Buenos Aires, a tale related at Whitelocke's court-martial with some bitterness. As he marched into the streets of the city Craufurd could not have known that the result of his attack was to have a profound bearing on the rest of his army career. A disappointed and frustrated man, borne out of the experience of having seen many junior officers promoted over his head, 'the conspiracy of mediocrity,' Craufurd was fiercely determined to do well in the attack and prove himself fit for higher command. Tragically, it was not to be and he would be left even more embittered.

Craufurd sent orders to Guard, with the 45th Regiment at the Residencia, to come and support him with a small detachment of that regiment, leaving Nicholls to hold his position with the main body of the 45th. Guard duly set off and met with little resistance other than that from a couple of discharges of a heavy gun placed at the end of a street. As he neared the centre of the city, however, he found the tops of the houses crowded with the enemy who opened up a smart fire on his men. The men were out of breath and in a tight spot, it being almost impossible to advance further. Therefore, Guard drew his men into a street on his right and from here he saw Pack with some of the Light Battalion approaching the convent of Santa Domingo. Guard went to consult with Pack who, as he rightly thought, had gained, from his time spent in the city the previous year, a good local knowledge of the streets and would be able to advise him on the practicability of any further advance through the street leading to the main square.

It was Pack's view that Guard stood no chance at all of gaining the square without the loss of his detachment and even as he spoke the two men looked up the street to see Craufurd, with several companies of light infantry and riflemen, together with a field piece, coming along the street towards them. Pack urged Craufurd to retreat to the Residencia after informing him of the sorry state of his column and of the impossibility of taking the city. Craufurd thought for a moment but then said it was his intention to remain at the convent and Pack reluctantly gave in and decided to stay with him.

The small field piece promptly blew in the door and the British troops rushed into the convent to find, much to the delight of Pack and a light company of the 71st Regiment, that the colours of that regiment, captured from, Beresford the previous year, were laid up there.

> We came to the church of St. Domingo, where the colours of the 71st Regiment had been placed as a trophy over the shrine of the Virgin Mary. We made a sally into it, and took them from that disgraceful resting place, where they had remained ever since the surrender of General Beresford to General Liniers.[7]

The colours were quickly hoisted above the convent as the green jacketed riflemen of the 95th threw themselves into positions in doors, windows and in the convent's tower. Spanish sharpshooters on the tops of the surrounding buildings soon opened up on the position but in spite of it Craufurd had no reason to be alarmed. He assumed all was well elsewhere in the city with the British attack and thought this to be all the more true when at about midday a Spanish officer approached the convent with a flag of truce, which Craufurd naturally thought was an offer by him to surrender. One can imagine his shock and surprise, therefore, when the officer gave him the stunning news that the British attack had been a total failure, that the 88th with Duff and Vandeleur, had surrendered and that it was he, in fact, who was calling on Craufurd to surrender. The British commander could hardly believe it and rejected the summons immediately. He was determined to fight on and get his men out at the first favourable opportunity.

At length, a large body of enemy troops was seen approaching the convent apparently with the intention of capturing the field piece which was still out in the street and which the British had been unable to drag inside, it being under fire from Spanish sharpshooters on the roofs. Craufurd quickly ordered down the riflemen from the different parts of the building in order to cover the evacuation of the post. The colours of the 71st were also taken down. The enemy had closed in, however, and were on the point of seizing the gun when, with a great yell, a grenadier company of the 45th under Guard, and a small party of light infantry under Major Trotter, charged them to prevent it being carried off. The Spaniards gave way but so heavy was the musketry from the houses and roofs that about forty of the 45th were either killed or wounded in the space of a few minutes. The enemy were reinforced by some *Minones* and *Patricios* who brought with them their own gun. These troops took the British in the rear and a fierce struggle ensued as they battled their way back to the convent. In the hacking and flaying that followed, Major Trotter was killed and the 3-pounder given up. Guard, with the rest of the party, regained the convent but left many of their comrades dead in the street.

It was now impossible for Craufurd to evacuate his men but he decided to keep up the fight as long as he could. He was known to have a violent temper, a fact proved particularly correct during the Peninsular War, and as it became obvious to him that no steps were being taken to support him he quickly got into a rage and was furious with Whitelocke, blaming him for his predicament. It is widely believed that he gave his men orders to shoot the commander-in-chief should any of them see him.

Whilst the British troops were pinned down inside the convent the Spaniards brought up a gun which opened fire from the courtyard of a house nearby, battering the convent tower and showering the British inside with dust and splinters whilst musket balls smacked continuously against the walls. The dead and wounded lay everywhere, out in the street and on the floor inside. It was a desperate situation. The sound of firing had ceased elsewhere in the city and from this Craufurd concluded that the attacks by the other British columns had failed. At about half-past three in the afternoon Craufurd called together Pack, Guard and Major MacLeod, who commanded the riflemen, and told them that it would be impossible to extricate themselves by their own efforts and that as the firing in all the other parts of the city had ceased they must assume that the attack had failed and that they were on their own.

> I told them that in my opinion a retreat was utterly impossible; that it was completely in the enemy's power to annihilate the remainder of the brigade, we being then with about 600 men in the very heart of the town, out of which it was clear to me that all the rest of the army had been obliged to retreat.[8]

After 'mature deliberation' it was decided that the only course open to them was to surrender and shortly after half-past three in the afternoon they held out a white flag and a Spanish officer came forward to accept it. In all, Craufurd's men numbered about six hundred rank and file, including a hundred of Guard's men and about seventy of Pack's. About a hundred were left on the floor of the convent, too badly wounded to be moved, whilst the rest were marched off as prisoners of war.

With the surrender of Craufurd's brigade at the convent of Santa Domingo the last serious fighting in Buenos Aires on 5 July ended. The only other units involved in the attack on the city that day were the 6th Dragoon Guards and the 9th Light Dragoons. These troops fought on foot armed with carbines and were under the command of Colonel Kington. They arrived at the entrance to the city at about seven in the morning and were preceded on the march by a small field gun. The dragoons advanced in an eerie silence and had got as far as a couple blocks without being shot at. From this point on, however, the firing started and by the time they had gone as far as the fourth block of houses the firing had become quite destructive. Encumbered by their heavy boots the dragoons tried to push on but such was the ferocity of the Spanish opposition that they were soon forced to a standstill. Pinned down and unable to break into any of the houses they were an easy target for the defenders concealed on the rooftops. Here, Kington and Captain Burrell were both killed, cut down in a hail of lead. With Kington dead Major Pigot, of the 9th Light Dragoons, was left with no choice but to order the column to retreat to the spot from which it had originally begun its attack. This was duly accomplished but not without loss and having achieved nothing whatsoever.

At this point we must take a look and see just exactly what Whitelocke had been doing all day. In fact, he had spent the best part of the day with Gower and the officers of his staff at the Corrale and had not moved an inch all day. He could hear the fighting going on in the city but had no idea how the attack was progressing and as the day wore on he grew more and more anxious. He had received not a single report from any of his commanders. In any case, they did not know where he was until eventually, at half-past four in the afternoon, he received his first report of the action. He had, however, tried to send an aide down one of the streets to try and see what was going on. This was at nine o'clock in the morning, three hours after the attack had begun. This proved totally useless, however, for in the gloomy morning haze it was impossible to see any great distance. Whitelocke then decided to send forward the 6th Dragoon Guards and the 9th Light Dragoons again who, as we have seen, had already been forced to withdraw to a spot nearby where they had originally started their attack. This time they moved up to the first square in the city where once again they were met by a heavy fire from all around them, forcing them to take up a position in some houses where they settled down to await developments.

Presently, one of Whitelocke's aides arrived at the position held by the dragoons and climbed on to a roof in an effort to see what was going on in the city. He then reported back to the Commander-in-Chief to tell him that he could see the flag of the 71st Regiment along with some riflemen on top of the convent of Santa Domingo and that the British flag was also flying above the Plaza de Toros to the left and on the Residencia to the right. This encouraged Whitelocke to send another aide, Samuel Whittingham, to try and make his way to Auchmuty to ascertain his position. Whittingham returned at a round half-past four, just as darkness was beginning to fall, to give Whitelocke his first real report on the day's action, a full seven and a half hours after the attack had been launched.

Whittingham reported that Auchmuty had been successful but that the 88th had surrendered. Of the other columns, however, there was no news at all. Captain Whittingham also delivered a request from Auchmuty to

Whitelocke asking the latter to move his headquarters to the Plaza de Toros but as it was now dark the Commander-in-Chief decided to wait until morning before moving or issuing orders.

It had been a thoroughly disjointed attack and at the end of a day which had seen the superiority of the British army neutralised by its having to fight in the streets of the Spaniards' own capital; we must stop to take a look at the situations of the various British columns.

The 88th Regiment, with two wings under Duff and Vandeleur, had been forced to surrender as had Craufurd's brigade along with Pack, Guard and Cadogan. The 6th Dragoon Guards and the 9th Light Dragoons occupied a position amongst some houses on the outskirts of the city. On the right, however, there had been some measure of success with the occupation of the Residencia by Major Nicholls and the 45th Regiment. We last saw Nicholls occupying this position, clearing away parties of enemy marksmen, whilst Guard took a small detachment of the regiment with him to join Craufurd. At about eleven o'clock Nicholls was relieved to see a British flag hoisted above a building about 800 yards from him. The Spaniards made no great effort to dislodge him but concentrated instead on the column occupying the building above which the flag was flying. This was actually Craufurd at the Santa Domingo. Nicholls grew more anxious when, at about three o'clock in the afternoon, the flag was lowered. This seemed to indicate that some misfortune had befallen them. In the meantime, however, he continued to strengthen his own position and sent out Captain Smith to clear the area around his position. Other parties were sent out likewise for the same purpose and every house seemed to contain armed persons who fired on the British soldiers at every opportunity but who made no resistance when the particular houses were forced. Many of these Spaniards escaped but the number of enemy killed or taken prisoner by the 45th was put at eighty. At nightfall all the men were ordered back inside the Residencia with the exception of three small outposts who were left in order to monitor the enemy's movements. These outposts had easy communication with the Residencia and were perfectly tenable. Their occupation that night also saved Nicholls the trouble of having to clear them the next day. This, then, was the situation on the right and centre of the British line.

Meanwhile, on the left, to the north of the city, the 36th Regiment, under Lumley, had met strong opposition and had been forced to join up with Auchmuty with the 38th and 87th Regiments at the Plaza de Toros. Lumley had sustained heavy losses whilst Auchmuty, in spite of the strong enemy resistance, had been relatively successful. Also at the Plaza de Toros was the 5th Regiment under King and Davie. The wounded men from this regiment were taken to a church nearby where they were put into the care of medical officers whilst elsewhere some unfortunate but familiar scenes were being re-enacted by some of the embattled British soldiers.

Shortly after the regiment had gone some of the twelve men left on guard went into a wine store close by, and two of them, from want of food and excitement, soon became intoxicated; and in attempting to cross the street in return to us were shot dead. To prevent a similar disaster the sergeant directed a sentry to be placed at the door of the wine house; and he too shared the fate of his comrades from the fire of a concealed enemy. The sergeant then took his station there; in a few seconds he also was a corpse.[9]

Darkness fell in Buenos Aires and apart from the odd crackle of musketry here and there as nervous men fired blindly into the shadows the fighting ceased. The British troops still in possession of their positions were able to get some sleep, rest or tend the wounded. All were exhausted and those unable to sleep were left to ponder on the day's events not really knowing how the other columns had fared or what the morning might bring. What they did know, however, was that the attack had not gone according to plan, that they still had not taken Buenos Aires and that something, somewhere, had gone drastically wrong.

VIII

Victory and Defeat

For Captain Samuel Whittingham the morning of 6 July was a busy one. At half-past six he was sent with an escort of ten cavalry and thirty infantry to find the British reserve under Colonel Mahon and order him to move at once to the Corrale del Miserere. Mahon himself had received orders to march on the 4th and on finding the bridge over the Rio Chuelo still intact and undefended had crossed it at five o'clock on the evening of the 5th, camping on the northern bank of the river just two miles from the Residencia. 'With the usual precautions,' said Whittingham,

> I advanced within half a mile of the Residencia, when, finding the enemy's parties falling back on the same point, and collecting in great numbers, I thought it right to endeavour to communicate to Colonel Mahon the order to advance to headquarters, before I attempted to force the road to the Residencia. I inclined, therefore, to the right, and in about half an hour fell in with the advanced pickets and waited upon the Colonel at his headquarters. With Colonel Mahon, I left the party of infantry I had brought with me, and received in return 100 men of the 40th Regiment, under the command of Captain Gilles.[1]

After delivering the orders Whittingham started out for the Residencia itself to ascertain just exactly what the position was on the British right. Major Nicholls, in command of the post, said he was sure he was capable of resisting the enemy's attempts to retake the place, but had no idea at all what had become of Craufurd's brigade. Even as the two officers consulted the Spanish renewed their attack on the place.

> Captain Whittingham arrived with an escort about 1 o'clock to procure intelligence for H.E. the Commander of the Forces,' recalled

113

Nicholls, 'which Major Tolley and myself were giving him from one of our out stations, when we received intelligence from Captain Drew, who commanded the advanced outpost, of the approach of a body of the enemy, which he soon repeated with the addition of their having cannon with them. No time was lost in forming the piquet, commanded by Major Lecky, and ordering a reinforcement from the interior; they amounted to eighty men and moved to the corner of the street to await the approach of the enemy and support Captain Drew's small detachment. When the enemy were at 300 yards' distance it was judged expedient to move on to meet them, which was rapidly done, Captain Drew joining us as had been previously agreed upon. In a very little time we reached the cannon, one of which they fired, but with such an elevation that we received no injury from it. The leading sections began to move slowly homewards with the howitzers, whilst the remainder pushed forward, to secure their limbers, which was also easily effected; the enemy halted when they found it was not our intention to advance further, and fired smartly up on our rear and flanks; they were, however, kept at a distance by Captain Bridge, whose company followed as a reserve from the Residencia and was ordered to cover our retreat. The enemy must have been much panic stricken at our approach, otherwise it would be difficult to account for our having but one man killed and five wounded in this affair. [2]

Having captured the two guns, therefore, Nicholls positioned one of them at a street corner to repel any future attacks whilst Whittingham returned to Whitelocke who was still at the Corrale waiting for news of the attack.

Meanwhile, inside the Fortress in Buenos Aires, Liniers and his officers were understandably elated at the success which they had achieved the previous day. With the capture of Craufurd, along with about two thousand other British soldiers, Liniers knew that British morale was bound to have been shaken and that the time was right to send Whitelocke an ultimatum summoning him to surrender. Liniers informed the civil and military leaders in Buenos Aires of his intention to send an ultimatum in which he would allow the British troops to re-embark along with the prisoners taken from Beresford the year before. He also stressed that should they try to attempt another attack then he could not guarantee the safety of the prisoners. Martin de Alzaga, however, was of the opinion that the terms were too generous and said that the British should be made to evacuate Montevideo also.

As all advantages are on our side, the enemy having suffered great losses, nothing could be gained if the English army would remain in Montevideo where in a few months, reinforced again, they will soon be masters of Buenos Aires. It is necessary to expel the enemy from Uruguay as a safety for the enemy.[3]

Liniers thought this might prevent the two sides from reaching an agreement but Alzaga insisted that the British army must agree to evacuate Montevideo. Consequently, a letter to that effect was written and signed by Liniers. It was sent to Whitelocke at daybreak on the 6th and was received by a British outpost at the Retiro. It was then passed on to Auchmuty who forwarded it to Whitelocke. The letter reached him at the Corrale just as he was about to move his headquarters to the Plaza de Toros to join Auchmuty.

Written in Spanish, the letter was translated by Captain Squire. In it Liniers stated that he had taken over two thousand prisoners who, to avoid further bloodshed, he would return, along with those taken from Beresford, on condition that the British re-embark and also evacuate Montevideo. He also said that in the event of Whitelocke refusing the terms he could not answer for the safety of the prisoners in view of the anger of his own troops who had become increasingly angry following the shooting of one of Liniers' aides who had been carrying a flag of truce. He added that he needed an answer within one hour. Whitelocke rejected the proposals but decided to reply to Liniers and suggest a truce of twenty-four hours in order to collect the wounded who were scattered in various parts of the city. This was really an attempt by Whitelocke to gain time but nevertheless his reply was delivered by Captain Brown who took with him an escort of twelve dragoons and forty infantry. Brown and his escort were fired upon repeatedly by the Spaniards but managed to make their way along the outskirts of the city to the Recoletas where Whitelocke's reply was given to Liniers. It read:

> I have to acknowledge the receipt of your letter, and you do me but justice in believing my sentiments in the cause of humanity. From the extent of the action, and the state of the wounded, I should propose a truce for twenty-four hours, the lines to remain as they now stand. As to surrendering as the army now is, it is quite out of the question, having taken so many prisoners. I have to lament your aide-de-camp being wounded; but these are casualties which are unavoidable; and I have to remark to you in return, that my aide-de-camp was fired at the whole way.[4]

Having rejected Liniers' proposals Whitelocke, together with Gower, an aide, an escort of dragoons and some artillery, left the Corrale at noon to join Auchmuty at the Plaza de Toros, leaving Colonel Bradford behind to await the arrival of Mahon. Whitelocke reached Auchmuty shortly afterwards and for the first time since the attack began at dawn the previous day he could consult personally and directly with one of his commanders on the state of the attack in that part, or for that matter, any part of the city. The three British generals, Whitelocke, Gower and Auchmuty then consulted upon the situation. Whitelocke estimated his losses to be around 2,500, killed, wounded and taken prisoner, but his guess was below the mark. Of the British troops that had taken part in the attack fifteen officers and 386 men had been killed, fifty-seven officers and 592 men wounded, and ninety-four officers and 1,831 men taken prisoner. Altogether, British losses were just twenty-five short of the three thousand mark, which represented a casualty rate of over fifty per cent.

On the other hand, however, Whitelocke could still consider himself to be in a strong position. After all, the British had captured over a thousand prisoners, over thirty guns and he was still in possession of two strong posts on either side of the city, namely the Plaza de Toros on the left and the Residencia on the right. Besides this he still had an effective fighting force of about six thousand men ready to continue the attack. But even as they consulted, the Spaniards resumed their own attacks on the British positions. Liniers had guessed that Whitelocke's request for a truce was just a ploy to gain time and he rejected it and resumed his attack instead. At the Residencia there was a notable movement of Spanish troops around the place which was held by the 45th Regiment and which had already been attacked an hour or so earlier.

> Between 2 and 3 o'clock intelligence was received as before, that the enemy was collecting with an apparent intention of attacking us a second time; a disposition to the former one was made, but they retired in disorder upon the first two discharges of the howitzer and did not trouble us again. Upon this last occasion the indiscreet zeal of men a few men tempted them to follow the enemy some 100 yards up the main street; they were, however, fortunate enough to rejoin us in safety.[5]

There was also renewed fighting at the Retiro where a piquet of the 87th drove off a large party of the enemy, capturing two officers and seventy men in the process. It soon became evident to both Gower and Auchmuty that the capture of Buenos Aires was impossible, especially with the lives of so many British prisoners at stake, should Whitelocke continue the attack. Therefore, the British commander-in-chief, on asking the two generals their opinion, was advised to enter into negotiations with Liniers. Whitelocke later explained the reasons behind his decision:

> General Liniers had likewise acquainted me in his letter that he could not answer for the lives of the British prisoners if the attack was persisted in. I have reason to believe that they would have been

sacrificed to the fury of an exasperated rabble. Nothing remained to be done offensively but another attack on the town similar to the last, the success of which must have been doubtful, as my forces when collected did not reach 5,000 men, and, even if successful, my losses would probably have rendered that force insufficient to hold the place when taken. With such a mass of armed inhabitants it would be impossible to control Buenos Aires until the arrival of additional support from the British army. If it was deemed fruitless to attempt another attack there yet remained two modes of retreat, either by treaty or re-embarking in the face of the enemy. The latter measure would certainly have been attended with additional loss and the wounded and prisoners as well as the 71st Regiment, in all 4,000 men, lost forever to Great Britain. In return for this I should have possessed but a nominal command of Montevideo, a post which can never be considered of any advantage, whilst the capital of the Provinces and the great entrepot of commerce (meaning Buenos Aires) remained in the hands of the enemy. By accepting the treaty the great point was gained of getting back all the prisoners, including those taken from Beresford. I should be enabled to bring off my own army almost entire and recover the 71st Regiment, a problem which my instructions have taught me to consider as of the first importance, and evacuate a province which the force I was authorised to calculate upon could never maintain, and which from the very hostile disposition of its inhabitants, was in truth not worth maintaining.[6]

Consequently, Gower was sent to Liniers with the following letter from Whitelocke:

I have the honour to inform Your Excellency that when I received your letter, I was coming to this place, and I presume from the renewal of artillery fire Your Excellency is not disposed to accept my proposition. It is most painful to me to witness the suffering of those who being wounded are in want of assistance and it is with this purpose that I propose to Your Excellency to cease fire and permit an officer of rank to explain to Your Excellency the terms which I propose to accept of those expressed in Your Excellency's former letter.[7]

As a result of this letter a suspension of hostilities was proclaimed at about four o'clock on the afternoon of the 6th. The cease fire was received with astonishment and disbelief by the various British units still in possession of their posts in the city.

Flags of truce were going in and out all day. We naturally enough imagined that although we had lost the Light Brigade and the 88th

Regiment, and especially as the enemy had kept close in their quarters, that they had sent to surrender. How astonished then were the whole army to find, after all their hopes and sufferings, that we were to have all our own men again, who were taken prisoners, as also the 71st Regiment, and to instantly embark! Grief, disgust, and execration were the sentiments of the moment, and we embarked shortly after, in sight of the enemy, that scarcely believed their eyes, and were anxious to get us on board as soon as possible. Nobody could conceive what the evacuation of Montevideo meant, as we could always embark when we pleased, and take plenty of the enemy's cannon with us; and with regard to prisoners, we have enough of them, so that they durst not have used our people ill.[8]

Meanwhile, Gower had received verbal instructions from Whitelocke relative to the points which he was to discuss with Liniers. Gower rode into the city with an escort of Spanish officers who had been taken prisoner to be used as hostages for the small British escort. They arrived at the Plaza Mayor and found it occupied by about 4,000 armed people who refused to recognise the flag of truce. They screamed abuse at Gower and his men and fired over their heads. Gower and his party were held up here for a short while before two mounted Spanish officers with some cavalry rode through the crowd to escort them to the Fortress where they were in turn shown to Liniers.

Whitelocke had instructed Gower to pay particular attention to the question of the possession of Montevideo. Liniers had proposed a British withdrawal within two months but Gower was told to press for six instead. He was also instructed to request that the British army be allowed to re-embark at whichever point it wished and with all its guns and stores, and any such as they had captured from the Spaniards that they might wish to take with them. Gower and Liniers had been discussing the proposals for a short time when the noise of the mob outside grew so loud that they had to stop in order to find out what was going on. As it happened, word had spread that Denis Pack, who had escaped from Buenos Aires earlier, had been taken again and was being held inside the Fortress where Liniers and Gower were negotiating the terms of surrender. The crowd were baying for Pack's blood as they considered him to have broken his parole, as one of Gower's escorts, Captain Fraser later recalled:

The avenues were crowded by the mob who were calling out for 'Signora Pack, Signora Pack', meaning Colonel Pack. General Liniers was at this time talking with some of the mob who had forced their way into the room where there were a number of British officers and the Spanish General at that moment seized one of the most turbulent of the mob by the neck and threatened him. General Liniers apparently explained in Spanish to the crowd who had broken into the room and they seemed in some measure tranquilized. There were at that time two or three priests standing about Colonel Pack's chair, I suppose for the purpose of protecting him. The party had been dining and the cloth had not yet been removed. I asked for a Spanish escort, which had now become absolutely necessary, and obtained it. On re-entering the courtyard going into the great square, I found the violence of the mob apparently very much increased; they insulted us in the same manner and I thought we should have fallen a sacrifice to their rage, and it was not without the greatest difficulty on the part of the Spanish escort, that we were allowed to go forward. It was dark before we reached headquarters.[9]

Pack was eventually sent back safely to the British lines disguised as a Spaniard in order to protect him from the mob.

When Gower returned to the Plaza de Toros he showed Whitelocke the notes taken down during his discussions. Liniers had insisted that the period of two months for the evacuation of Montevideo remain unchanged, at which Gower remarked that he did not think the Spanish general would change his mind. Gower also said he had tried to obtain better conditions but Liniers would not give an inch and he added that it was only with great difficulty that he had managed to persuade him to allow the British to remain in Montevideo for two months as Martin de Alzaga was pressing for one month. Whitelocke was left with no choice but to accept Liniers proposals and the next day, 7 July 1807, he and Admiral Murray, representing British authority on land and sea in South America, signed the treaty which effectively put an end to all British aspirations in that continent.

The main points of the treaty included the mutual exchange of prisoners, that the British be allowed to take with them any arms and supplies in their possession and that they re-embark from Buenos Aires within ten days and from Montevideo within two months, leaving behind the artillery captured there.

Thus terminated one of the most sanguinary conflicts Britons were ever engaged in, and all owing to the stupidity of the General-in-Chief and General Leveson-Gower. Liniers, a Frenchman by birth, who commanded, treated us prisoners tolerably well, but he had little to give us to eat, his citadel not being provisioned for a siege. We were three or four days in his hands, when, in consequence of the disgraceful convention entered into by General Whitelocke, who agreed within two months to evacuate the territory altogether and to give up the fortress of Montevideo, we were released.[10]

The exchange of prisoners began the next day starting with the release of the officers, followed by the other ranks who were freed on the 9th. Before releasing the British prisoners, however, the people of Buenos Aires carried out a thorough search of them in order to make sure that they left behind all of the plunder acquired by them during the attack:

> We were all searched and every article that was Spanish taken from us, but we were allowed to keep the rest. During the search one soldier, who had a good many doubloons, put them into his kettle, with flesh and water above them, placed all upon a fire and kept them safe. There were about one hundred of us, who had been taken in the church, marched out of prison to be shot, unless we produced a gold crucifix of great value that was missing. We stood in a large circle of Spaniards and Indians. Their level pieces and savage looks gave us little hopes unless the crucifix was produced. It was found on the ground, on the spot where we stood; but it was not known who had taken it. The troops retired, and we were allowed to go back to prison without further molestation.[11]

The British prisoners were not treated too badly by the Spaniards although many of them admitted to being somewhat concerned for their safety should the mob of angry people outside get out of control and turn on them.

> We were then marched into the citadel, where a hundred and five of us were crammed into two rooms, leading into each other; a motley group, sure enough, and we certainly looked monstrous queer. The first day we had little or nothing to eat, but a little tub of water was placed in the outer apartment, the object of which was not exactly understood by all. Some went to drink, some went to p—, and some went to drink again. The inner room was made the sleeping one, where each occupied as many bricks as his body covered, and no more. We lay down, not quite sure whether our throats would be cut during the night or not.[12]

The exchange of prisoners took place at the Retiro and on their way there the bitterly disappointed British soldiers passed heaps of their own dead comrades, all stripped and unburied. Whitelocke himself met a party of riflemen on their return to the British lines and welcomed them back, declaring that he had much uneasiness on their account, fearing for their safety. The riflemen said nothing.

Not all of the British prisoners were returned, however. It is said that a local woman named Martina Cespedes told Liniers that he had made a mistake in the total number of prisoners taken. She told him that together with her daughters she had shut up twelve English soldiers in her house. Each of the twelve had gone into the house for a drink and one by one had been shut up in the rooms after having their arms taken from them. She added that she would be returning only ten of them as her daughters had decided to marry the two they had captured themselves. Liniers and his staff were astonished by this but said that under the terms of the treaty all soldiers would have to be returned. Only ten did, however, as the woman said, 'we have foreseen your case; your lordship can count them among the dead as they do not wish to leave Buenos Aires!'[13]

The prisoners were glad to be released but they felt a great sense of frustration, shame and bitterness about the whole business and deeply resented the humiliation which they had suffered at the hands of Liniers' volunteer army. One can imagine the sense of shock and disbelief that must have overcome the British troops still in possession of key posts in the city when the news of the surrender came through since they were still confident in their ability to go on and capture the city. However, they were totally unaware of the full extent of the failure of the attack. Some of the officers, too, felt badly let down by Whitelocke. Indeed, the whole affair was said to have deeply embittered Robert Craufurd throughout the rest of his career.

One of the things that rankled uppermost in the minds of the British soldiers was that they had failed to overcome an army which they had considered to have been a rabble, and one which they would have easily defeated in the open field. Indeed, it was a great sense of frustration to them that they failed to induce the Spaniards to fight in the open.

The slogan, 'General Whitelocke is a coward, a traitor or both' was scribbled on the walls of Buenos Aires by the British soldiers as they pulled back from their positions to begin the re-embarkation aboard the ships that would take them to Montevideo and then home. The re-embarkation began on 10 July from the northern end of the city and with the exception of those too badly wounded to be moved, who were left behind with some English surgeons, the whole force was re-embarked by 12 July. The British ships were about a mile distant from the shore, the river being too shallow to get in close. To reach them the officers and men were forced to wade waist deep through the water, just as they had done just a couple of weeks before when, amidst high spirits and much optimism, they had landed to begin the second attack on Buenos Aires.

When the ships reached Montevideo they found crowds of eager merchants waiting for them, merchants who had come out to South America to make their fortunes. They were expecting to hear the good news that Buenos Aires, the new *El Dorado*, was safely in British hands. Instead, however, they were given the shocking news of the failure of Whitelocke's expedition, news that was greeted by them with deep despair. Hundreds of people who had staked their all in a bid to cash in on the enormous potential that the colonies of the Rio de la Plata offered as a market for British goods found themselves ruined. Indeed, ever since Popham's circular the previous year following Beresford's capture of Buenos Aires frantic efforts had been made by merchants who were desperate to open up and exploit the new markets of South America, whilst along with them came other people from all walks of life hoping to cash in on the enterprise. They had brought with them on their long and often dangerous journey all sorts of goods, mainly worthless rubbish which they were unable to sell anywhere else. But now, these people and all the other merchants found they had tons of such stuff on their hands and with the British defeat found they were unable to sell to anybody. Many of them were consequently ruined and there were calls for an immediate inquiry into the conduct of the campaign.

The British army itself did not remain long in Montevideo but evacuated the place within the specified two month period. The army returned to England leaving behind them the dreams of a South American conquest. Samuel Whittingham later summed up the feelings of the British troops when he wrote:

History will record, and posterity with difficulty will believe, that such an army as ours capitulated with the rabble of a South American town, and sold the interests of the country, and gave up the hard-earned conquests of their brother soldiers, in order to secure a retreat which it was most amply in their power to have made of their good pleasure; or, at best, to procure that liberty for their countrymen which under such circumstances was scarcely worth their acceptance. But enough of this subject. I am sick of it! Would to God the waters of Oblivion were as near at hand as are those of La Plata.[14]

IX

Aftermath

News of the disastrous end to the campaign in South America reached London on 16 September 1807. The level of expectation of the campaign was so high that when the news broke there followed a storm of fury and anger which was directed almost totally at Whitelocke who was to be made a scapegoat for the whole affair. Greedy British merchants felt they had been cheated of their spoils and the soldiers' chances of success thwarted by the inept performance of their commanding officer. All this was reflected and often greatly exaggerated in numerous reports and eye-witness pamphlets that appeared on the streets. The only conclusion the people could come to was that Whitelocke deserved the same treatment which the luckless Admiral Byng had received some years before: he deserved to be shot. There were loud cries for an inquiry until eventually, in January 1808, Whitelocke was brought before a court martial and put on trial.

President of the Court, a strong one, was Sir William Meadows, and among the nineteen other members were David Dundas and Henry Fox and Lieutenant-Generals Cathcart, Lake, Hams and Sir John Moore. There were four lengthy charges. First, that Whitelocke, by his excessive demands made upon the people of Buenos Aires at a time when it looked as though they might come to terms, only served to increase the spirit of resistance in the people of the city. Second, that he badly mishandled the whole operation against Buenos Aires and that he had no right to order the men to attack with their muskets unloaded. Third, that he made no attempt whatsoever to support the attacking columns, and fourth, that he had shamefully abandoned the cities of Buenos Aires and Montevideo when in possession of the latter and in a strong position to carry the former.

The trial lasted thirty-one days during which the Court listened to evidence given by nearly all the officers who had taken part in the campaign and who had survived. As it dragged on, the full extent of the gross mismanagement of the whole campaign by Whitelocke and, to a greater extent Gower, unfolded. One problem was that Whitelocke was not used to command on service, and the fact that he had with him an inexperienced staff did not help matters. As a result he became edgy and anxious in trying to ensure that his orders were being carried out correctly. An experienced staff would have been able to foresee a good deal of its commander's wishes and would have anticipated his orders. This could have removed the friction that existed throughout the campaign.

The march from Ensenada highlighted these problems. The progress was painfully slow; thirty-one miles in four days, sixteen in the first three. The troops were continually harassed and hurried along and as a result they were never really able to halt long enough to cook themselves a decent meal, that is if they were fortunate enough to find anything substantial to eat, most of the supplies of food and water having been swallowed up in the swamp. Whitelocke's orders were not issued in proper time and the marches usually began late in the day. We have already seen the bad conditions in which the troops had to march, exposed as they were to the storms and pouring rain without any shelter at all, and with deep marshes, cuts and rivulets proving a continual hindrance and causing frequent halts along the way. All this could have been avoided if Whitelocke had sent an officer across from Montevideo to reconnoitre the countryside around Ensenada before the landings took place.

The lack of cavalry was also a major factor in the failure of the campaign. Communications between Gower, with the vanguard, and Whitelocke with the main body of the army were extremely poor. Indeed, had Whitelocke been in touch with Gower on 2 July following the fight at the Corrale there is little doubt that Craufurd would have been allowed to push on and capture Buenos Aires that very night whilst the defending Spanish forces were still scattered and disorganised.

Whitelocke tried to defend himself as best he could by trying to lay the blame for the failure of the assault at the feet of Craufurd and Pack. Here he did have some grounds for complaint since Craufurd was often reluctant to obey any order which did not meet with his personal approval. Indeed, his refusal to withdraw to the Residencia on Pack's advice after the failure of the latter's own attack illustrates this only too well. To be fair to Craufurd, however, it also has to be said that his own orders were none too clear. In fact, an important clause concerning the action to be taken in the event of meeting strong opposition was omitted from his copy of the 'Order for Attack' and as such he was unaware of Whitelocke's instructions.

The trial dragged on with witnesses giving their own detailed versions of the events of the campaign and with Craufurd and other officers arguing as though Whitelocke, or for that matter Gower, had actually formed a plan of attack. The truth was, however, that there never really was one. The British troops were simply divided into thirteen different columns and then thrust into thirteen different streets leaving the rest to chance. It was as though Whitelocke had expected a repeat of Beresford's entry into the city the year before when he encountered hardly any resistance at all. This, possibly, was the biggest mistake the British made; that of underestimating the Spanish forces and the peoples' will to resist. As one Spanish general was later quoted as saying:

Half the number of troops which attacked this capital would make themselves masters of it, supposing the same defenders, equally armed and disciplined I will rather say that ten thousand English sheep came to present their throats to the knife.[1]

The trial also illustrated the role played by Gower of whom it was later said, 'was as conceited as he was impractical, as overbearing as he was incompetent...the evil genius of the campaign.'[2] One can almost believe that he did his worst for Whitelocke, issuing verbal orders to some and not to others and generally adding confusion to the already confounded and bemused officers. Indeed, Sir Harry Smith, who was present at Buenos Aires, later wrote in his autobiography that Gower was the great culprit, the man who was to blame for the failure of the campaign. He called him an overbearing, disobedient man who ought to have been dismissed from the service, adding that Whitelocke was more abused than he deserved. Indeed, it could be said that Whitelocke had been placed in an impossible position from the outset. Even if he had been able to capture Buenos Aires he would have needed thousands of troops to keep possession of it. In the event, and following his defeat, he probably secured the best terms that he could expect in such a situation. His reasons for capitulating have already been perfectly stated by him in the previous chapter but certainly the fact uppermost in his mind would have been the danger that the lives of the British prisoners would have been placed in had he persisted with his attack on the 6th. He considered the lives of these men more important than the capture of a place which he thought Britain could never maintain, nor did he think it worth maintaining.

There was, of course, one other party that had a part to play in the British invasion of the Rio de la Plata, namely the British government, the 'Ministry of all the Talents'. After all, it was from here that Craufurd received his absurd orders concerning the conquest of South America. More important, it was the government that issued Whitelocke with his contradictory orders stating that he was to capture Buenos Aires by force yet also stated that he was not to distress or annoy the Spanish people. To be fair to the ministers, however, it must be remembered that they had been committed to the venture ever since Popham's pirate-like raid on the city in 1806. He had gained public support for his bid to take the colonies, and popular pressure from this quarter, plus the temptation of being able to neutralise Napoleon's blockade by opening up new, lucrative markets in South America, had forced the government's hand. They acted, however, in complete ignorance of the true situation in the Rio de la Plata and as such their gamble failed.

Popham himself was recalled in disgrace and tried before a Court Martial but he got off extremely lightly considering the fact that it was he who started the whole business in the first place. Although he was given a severe reprimand he found himself employed again almost immediately. Whitelocke was not so lucky. The seething, enraged British public needed a scapegoat and it was Whitelocke that fitted the bill. One writer has since said of his trial that there is no fairer tribunal in the world than a British Court Martial but added that the senior British officers who made up the court, even though they desired nothing more than to exercise judicial power aright, could hardly help feeling a great sense of disappointment at the outcome of the campaign in the Rio de la Plata and at the humiliation suffered by the army, and consequently were not inclined to be as merciful as they might have been. If they had waited a while for public sentiment to subside the trial might have been held in an atmosphere more beneficial to Whitelocke, and, possibly, the British people might have been able to see just how difficult a situation he found himself in. Sadly for Whitelocke, it was not to be. He was found guilty on all charges except that part of the second which related to the troops having to attack with their arms unloaded and the prohibition of firing. The sentence of the court was that he be cashiered and declared totally unfit and unworthy to serve His Majesty in any military capacity whatsoever. The king himself ordered the sentence to be entered into every regimental orderly book and that it was to be read to every regiment as 'a lasting memorial of the fatal consequences to which officers expose themselves, who, in the discharge of the important duties confided to them, are deficient in that zeal.'[3] It was an unhappy end for Whitelocke of whom, and of the sentence itself, it was later said:

Generosity... is not a virtue common among Englishmen, and the unhappy man, after his condemnation, existed for a quarter of a century, every day of which must have been a living death.[4]

Whitelocke quickly became the subject of many cartoons and caricatures ridiculing his conduct during the campaign and he died an unhappy man in 1833. He was buried in Bristol cathedral where his grave is marked simply 'John Whitelocke, Esq, resident of Clifton, died October 1833.'

Whitelocke was to be the sole scapegoat for the whole affair as none of the other officers who took part in the campaign in South America were disciplined, although Gower was never again given any worthwhile command. In fact, many of the officers rose to great heights later in their army careers, most notably Robert Craufurd, who rose to almost legendary status in the Peninsular War under Moore and then Wellington before dying a hero's death at the storming of Ciudad Rodrigo in January 1812. Other officers who fought in the campaign and achieved great fame in the Peninsula and at Waterloo and afterwards, included Harry Smith, victor of Aliwal, Cadogan, a hero of Vittoria, Denis Pack, and, of course, Beresford, who became one of Wellington's most trusted generals and who was to be the victor of Albuera.

There were many more besides and it is when we consider the list of future notables that the failure of the British army at Buenos Aires becomes all the more astonishing. But for all the British officers who took part in the campaign in the Rio de la Plata it was an episode in their careers best forgotten about. Indeed, it was destined to become one of the more obscure campaigns ever undertaken by the British army.

The people of the city of Buenos Aires meanwhile celebrated their triumph by giving thanks to the 'God of Victories'. Those who had fallen fighting in the streets were awarded full military honours at their funerals and pensions were given to their widows and orphans. The recapture of the city in 1806 was to become known as *La Reconquista* and the defence the following year *La Defensa*. Liniers was awarded the rank of Marshal and all his officers received commissions for the military ranks with which they had assisted in the defence of the city. Many of the names of the streets and plazas were changed in remembrance of the two victories, the streets being named after those who had died fighting or who had been a commander. Streets were also named after members of the Cabildo.

The campaign proved disastrous to the British army, but for the people of the viceroyalty of the Rio de la Plata it was to be the beginning of the road to independence. Indeed, the defeat of the British army marked the awakening of a nation, for having shaken off the old colonial government of the viceroy, Sobremonte, soon after the *Reconquista* the population suddenly realised just how much power they really had. They had deposed the viceroy, elected their own leader, Liniers, and now had a new army, and with the inspiration of the victory over the British behind them they were soon ready to challenge Spain itself.

In 1810 the people of Buenos Aires rebelled against the established Spanish government and soon the free nation of Argentina was born. It was ironic, however, that Liniers, who had done so much to defend the colony against the British in 1806 and 1807 and who had stirred in the people such a great nationalistic pride and feeling, now found himself a victim of this very same power. He remained loyal to Spain throughout the rebellion of 1810 and even tried to stage a counter-revolution in Cordoba. It failed, however, and he tried to escape to Peru. But before he could reach safety he was captured and sentenced to be taken to Buenos Aires to be shot. He never reached the city, however, for the escort from Cordoba decided to carry out the execution on the way, and on 10 August 1810, Liniers, together with some other loyalists, was shot by a firing squad by the roadside in a lonely wood. It was a sad end for the man who only a short time before had been acclaimed as a hero by the people of Buenos Aires.

In spite of the two British invasions relations between Britain and Argentina prospered. Both Pack and Beresford sent gifts to the people of Buenos Aires in remembrance of the humane treatment given to the wounded after the fighting that had taken place in the city during both invasions. Links between the two countries also flowered as a result of the personal relationships formed between the men captured by Liniers after Beresford's invasion in 1806 and the local people in the towns where they were held as prisoners of war. One such town was Mendoza, capital of the province of Cuyo. British prisoners were held here between 1806 and 1807 but when the order of repatriation came through after Whitelocke's surrender a great many of them refused to leave. They settled and married although their surnames have disappeared over the years. Some of the British troops later returned to South America to fight as the British Legion under Simon Bolivar during the Wars of Independence, which is somewhat ironic as it was just such a request from Miranda, that is, British aid for the patriots, that sparked Popham into starting off the British invasions in the first place although the troops under Bolivar, it must be said, were not regulars but were recruited as mercenaries by South American agents.

It is strange to relate that just as a great number of British troops ended up fighting for Argentina in the Wars of Independence, a group of six hundred Uruguayans saw service in the Peninsular War fighting on the side of Britain. These Uruguayans, or more accurately, inhabitants of Banda Oriental, had been taken prisoner in February 1807, following Auchmuty's capture of Montevideo. They were then transported to England and kept in captivity in the old hulks that were moored on the River Thames. Most of the prisoners were from the Regiment Blandenques de la Frontera, the Regiment Fijo de Buenos Aires and the Dragones de Buenos Aires. Along with these troops there was the governor of Montevideo, Ruiz Huidobro, and Generals Rondeau, Zapiola, Vasquez, Zufriategun and Jimerez de Arechaga.

Following the agreement made by Whitelocke after his capitulation these troops were sent to Spain. They were transported in different ships but were re-united in Corunna, the capital of Galicia. Here they took the name of the Battalion de Buenos Aires and formed part of the garrison until war against France was declared. The battalion was dressed in short red jackets with white waistcoats and trousers. By an amazing coincidence these uniforms had been taken from an English frigate, the *Elisa,* which had been captured by none other than Santiago Liniers many years before during his days in the Spanish navy. It was as a result of this action that Liniers was made a captain. Soon the battalion changed its name and became known as 'the Colorados.' When the Peninsular War broke out the Colorados formed part of the 1st Division of the Army of Castile, which was commanded by General Joachim Blake. Soon afterwards they joined General Cuesta and his Army of Galicia and they were soon in action against the French. On 14 July 1808, on the plains of Medina del Rio Seco, the armies of Galicia, Asturias and Castile faced up to the Imperial French Corps of Bessieres, Mauton, Lasalle, Merle and Sabathier. The battle lasted nearly all day and although the Spaniards were completely defeated the Colorados of Buenos Aires fought fiercely against their French enemies. After this battle Blake formed a mounted unit from the remains of the Colorados called the 'Dragones del General'. These were dressed like the gauchos back in Argentina and were even armed with lassos and bolas. This force took part in the siege of Astorga and in the victory at Tamames for which the officers all received gold commemorative medals. Their last action took place at Ciudad Rodrigo where Rondeau received his commission. On this occasion the troops from the Rio de la Plata came directly under Wellington's command. When the Peninsular War ended the Dragones del General returned to Montevideo after their adventures in England and Spain which had kept them away from their homeland for seven years.

There were two coincidences relating to South American soldiers serving in the Peninsular War, one of which concerned the most famous Argentine soldier of all, San Martin, who led his country to independence and who, along with Simon Bolivar, was mainly responsible for the defeat of Spain in South America. San Martin was present at the second siege of Badajoz, in Spain, in 1811, when the town was being besieged by an Anglo-Portuguese army under the command of William Beresford, captor of Buenos Aires in 1806. The other also concerns Beresford who whilst in command of the Portuguese army in the Peninsula met up with one of his former adversaries from 1806, General Elio, who was also serving with the Portuguese army.

The Reconquista and La Defensa were not simply cases of a volunteer army defeating a British army but were events that were to prove an inspiration and springboard to independence. The feeling of the time is summed up in a poem written by a young captain of Patricios who, invoking the spirits of those who died in the Defensa wrote:

…Vuestros hechos
Serviran a mas gloria de incentivo
…alli al nino

Sus padres llevaran, y electrizados
Le diran: aqui posa el heroismo.
Al tierno pecho pasara la llama
Que alimento los vuestros, y principio
Tendra alli sur valor: he ahi los frutos
Que daries a la patria: he ahi los hijos
Que a la patria daran vuestras cenizas.

Freely translated this means:

...Thus shall your deeds
A spur to future glory prove.
...There the parents
Their stripling sons shall bring and say,
Here lie the heroes of your land!
The fires that warmed those breasts of thine
Shall flame in their young bosoms then,
Nor shall burn in vain.
Behold! the fruits that ye your patria bore,
Behold! the sons that from your ashes soar.[5]

From Britain's point of view we can only reflect and ponder upon what might have been had Whitelocke managed to capture and hold on to Buenos Aires. Would Britain have settled for the colony of the Rio de la Plata or would she have tried to advance to take possession of other Spanish territories in South America? Nobody knows. What we do know is that the defeat of British arms kindled a flame which sparked off a blaze of nationalistic fervour in the people of Buenos Aires, which in turn inspired the birth of a new nation, Argentina, a flame which would also free her from the yoke of Old Spain and ultimately drive the Spanish from South America altogether.

Appendices

Appendix I

A Summary of Statistics, Troop Numbers, Casualties, etc.

Beresford's Landing Force, Point de Quilmes, 25 June 1806.
Staff 7, R. Engineers 3, Royal Artillery 36, St. Helena Artillery 102, 20th Light Dragoons 7, 71st Regiment 844, St. Helena Infantry 182, Marines 340, Seamen 100,
Officers 70.
Total: 1,641.

Casualties, Buenos Aires, 12 August 1806.
2 officers, 46 men killed,
8 officers, 99 men wounded,
10 men missing.
Total: 165.

Backhouse's force.
Royal Artillery 6, 38th Regiment 811, 47th Regiment 685, 54th Regiment 103, 20th Light Dragoons 191, 21st Light Dragoons 140, Officers, sgts 244.
Total: 2,180.

Auchmuty's force.
40th Regiment 1000, 87th Regiment 826, 95th Regiment 300, Royal Artillery 170, 17th Light Dragoons 700 (Dismounted)
Total: 2,996.

Craufurd's force.
5th Regiment 836, 36th Regiment 822, 45th Regiment 850, 88th Regiment 798, 95th Regiment 364, Royal Artillery 243, 6th Dragoon Guards 299, Officers, sgts, 588.
Total: 4,800.

Whitelocke's force.
Horse Artillery 130 (Dismounted), 89th Regiment 1000 *, Draft of recruits 500.
Total: 1,630.

* The 89th sailed separately and did not arrive in time to take part in the action.

Casualties, Buenos Aires, 5 July. 1807.
15 officers, 386 men killed
57 officers, 597 men wounded
94 officers, 1,831 men prisoners
Total: 2,325 all ranks

Prisoners taken by the Spaniards, 5 July 1807.
Royal Artillery 20, 6th Dragoon Guards 2, 95th Regiment 560, Light Battalion 809, 88th Regiment 451, 45th Regiment 82.
Total: 1,924.

Return of Spanish prisoners taken between 2-5 July 1807.
At the Plaza de Toros 700, At the Corralle 200, At the Residencia 100.
Total: 1,000 (approx).

Return of the effective British force after the attack on the city of Buenos Aires, 5 July 1807.
Royal Navy 217, Royal Artillery 311, Gunners, drivers, 113, 6th Dragoon Guards 281, 9th Light Dragoons 593, 17th Light Dragoons 641, 5th Regiment 743, 36th Regiment 682, 38th Regiment 519, 40th Regiment 823, 45th Regiment 567, 47th
Regiment 68, 87th Regiment 501.
Total: 6,059.

Appendix II

**Proceedings of a General Court Martial Held at Chelsea Hospital,
Upon Charges Exhibited against Lieutenant-General Whitelocke,
Thursday, 28 January 1808.**

FIRST CHARGE. That Lieutenant-General Whitelocke, having received instructions from His Majesty's principal Secretary of State to proceed for the reduction of the province of Buenos Aires, pursued measures ill calculated to facilitate that conquest; that when the Spanish commander had shown such symptoms of a disposition to treat, as to express a desire to communicate with Major-General Gower, the second in command, upon the subject of terms, the said Lieutenant-General Whitelocke did return a message, in which he demanded, amongst other articles, the surrender of all persons holding civil offices in the government of Buenos Aires, as prisoners of war; that the said Lieutenant-General Whitelocke in making such an offensive and unusual demand, tending to exasperate the inhabitants of Buenos Aires, to produce and encourage a spirit of resistance to His Majesty's arms, to exclude the hope of amicable accommodation, and to increase the difficulties of the service with which he was trusted, acted in a manner unbecoming his duty as an officer, prejudicial to military discipline, and contrary to the Articles of War.

SECOND CHARGE. That the said Lieutenant-General Whitelocke, after the landing of the troops at Ensenada, and during the march from thence to the town of Buenos Aires, did not make the military arrangements best calculated to ensure the success of his operations against the town, and that having known, previously, to his attack upon Buenos Aires upon the 5th of July, 1807, as appears from his public despatch of the 10th July, that the enemy meant to occupy the flat roofs of the houses, he did nevertheless, in the said attack, divide his force into several brigades and parts, and ordered the whole to be unloaded, and no firing to be permitted on any account; and, under this order, to march into the principal streets of the town unprovided with proper and sufficient means for forcing the barricades, whereby the troops were unnecessarily exposed to destruction, without the possibility of making effectual opposition; such conduct betraying great professional incapacity on the part of the said Lieutenant-General Whitelocke, tending to lessen the confidence of the troops in the judgement of their officers, being derogatory to the honour of His Majesty's arms, contrary to his duty as an officer, prejudicial to good order and military discipline and contrary to the Articles of War.

THIRD CHARGE. That the said Lieutenant-General Whitelocke did not make, although it was in his power, any effectual attempt, by his own personal exertion or otherwise, to co-operate with, or support, the different divisions of the army under his command, when engaged with the enemy in the streets of Buenos Aires on the 5th July, 1807; whereby those troops, after having encountered and surmounted a constant and well directed fire, and having effected the purport of their orders, were left without aid and support, or further orders, and considerable detachments under Lieutenant-Colonel Duff and Brigadier General Craufurd were thereby compelled to surrender; such conduct on the part of the said Lieutenant-General Whitelocke tending to the defeat and dishonour of His Majesty's arms, to lessen the confidence of the troops in the skill and courage of their officers, prejudicial to good order and military discipline, and contrary to the Articles of War.

FOURTH CHARGE. That the said Lieutenant-General Whitelocke, subsequent to the attack on the town of Buenos Aires, and at a time when the troops under his command were in possession of posts on each flank of the town, and of the principal arsenal, with a communication open to the fleet, and having an effective force of upwards of 5000 men, did enter into, and finally conclude, a treaty with the enemy, whereby he acknowledges in the public despatch of the 10th of July, 1807, 'That he resolved to forego the advantages which the bravery of his troops had obtained, and which advantages had cost him about 2500 men in killed, wounded and prisoners;' and by such treaty he unnecessarily and shamefully surrendered all such advantages, totally evacuated the town of Buenos Aires, and consented to deliver, and did shamefully abandon and deliver, up to the enemy the strong fortress of Montevideo, which had been committed to his charge, and which, at the period of the treaty and abandonment, was well and sufficiently garrisoned and provided against attack, and which was not, at such period, in a state of blockade or siege; such conduct on the part of the said Lieutenant-General Whitelocke tending to the dishonour of His Majesty's arm's, and being contrary to his duty as an officer, prejudicial to good order and military discipline, and contrary to the Articles of War.

Appendix III

General Whitelocke's Sentence.

Horse Guards, March 24th, 1808.

SENTENCE. The Court Martial having duly considered the evidence given in support of the Charges against the prisoner, Lieutenant-General Whitelocke, his defence, and the evidence he has adduced, are of the opinion, that he is guilty of the whole of the said Charges, with the exception of that part of the Second Charge which related to the order that 'the columns should be unloaded, and that no firing should be permitted on any account.'

The Court are anxious that it may be distinctly understood, that they attach no censure whatever to the precautions taken to prevent any unnecessary firing during the advance of the troops to the proposed points of attack, and do therefore acquit Lieutenant-General Whitelocke of that part of the said Charge.

The Court adjudge, that the said Lieutenant-General Whitelocke be cashiered, and declared totally unfit, and unworthy to serve His Majesty in any military capacity whatever.

Appendix IV

A Note on Liniers' Volunteer Army.

When Beresford's invasion of 1806 began the available Spanish troops consisted mainly of regular units, the *Dragones de Buenos Aires* and the *Fijo de Buenos Aires*. These troops fared miserably against the British but helped during the *Reconquista* to defeat them. Following Beresford's surrender, however, it was obvious that new regiments would have to be formed to fight off further British reinforcements that were known to be on their way.

Having led the people to victory over the British in August, 1806, Liniers knew he would need volunteers to fight again and also to maintain his new position, the people of Buenos Aires having chosen him as their leader in place of the unpopular viceroy, the Marquis de Sobremonte. On 6 September, therefore, the *Chief of Arms* published a proclamation calling upon the population to arm themselves in view of the threat posed by the British whose ships were still moored in the river.

The order was given to the 'European' Spaniards, or *peninsulares*, that is to say those immigrants living in Buenos Aires, to form themselves into units according to the Spanish province of their origin. In this way Liniers' 'New Army' began to take shape. The *peninsulares* formed themselves into five regiments:

Cuerpo de Gallegos. One battalion of one grenadier and eight fusilier companies. 600 men in all, commanded by Pedro Andres Cervino.

Tercio de Andaluces. One battalion of eight companies, 55 men in each. Commanded by Jose Merello.

Minones de Cataluna. One battalion of eight companies with 75 men in each. Organised by Jaime Nadal y Guarda and commanded by Olaguer Reynals.

Tercio de Vizcainos. Eight companies, 60 men in each. Commanded by Prudencio Murguiondo.

Tercio de Montaneses. Four companies of 50 men each. Formed by Jose de La Oyuela and later commanded by Pedro Andres Garcia.

In spite of these new regiments Liniers felt he would need more troops to defend Buenos Aires from further attack. A royal order dating from February 1795 stated that the viceroy could only impose emergency measures for defence in conjunction with a *junta de guerra*, or council of war, which should consist of the Intendant and senior officers of the garrison. Liniers, therefore, formed the *junta* which enabled him to create the volunteer corps that would form his new army. The existing militia in Buenos Aires was greatly strengthened by volunteers and from this the various regiments and battalions were formed:

Cavalry:

1st Escuadron de Husares, (Husares de Pueyrredon). Formed by Juan Martin de Pueyrredon but commpnded by Martin Rodriguez when the former travelled to Spain to represent the *Cabildo* of Buenos Aires. Four squadrons, totalling 200 men. The regiment also supplied 204 men to fight on foot.

2nd Escuadron de Husares, (Husares de Vivas). Named after its commander, Lucas Vivas, a proprietor in Buenos Aires, this regiment numbered some 186 men.

3rd Escuadron de Husares, (Husares de Nunez). Numbering 181 men, this regiment was named after its commander, Pedro Ramon Nunez, a native of Spain.

Cazadores de la Reina, (4th Husares). Formed in November, 1806, by Diego de Herrera, this regiment numbered 200 men.

Migueletes de Castex. Numbering some 193 men, this regiment, formed by Doctor Alejo Castex, acted as escort to Liniers. *Carabineros de Carlos IV.* Mounted on expensive horses and led by Lucas Fernandez, this regiment numbered 190 men. *Labradores y Quinteros.* Commanded by Antonio Luciano Ballester this regiment consisted of two squadrons, mainly farmers and agricultural workers from the rural areas.

Infantry:

Cuerpo de Patricios. The most famous of all Liniers' troops. Formed in September, 1806, the regiment consisted of three battalions each with eight battalions making 1359 men in all. The battalions were commanded by Correlio Saavedra, Esteban Romero and Jose Domingo de Urien, respectively. The regiment was composed entirely of *portenos*, natives of Buenos Aires and the officers were elected by ballot. The regiment is still in existence in Argentina today.

Cazadores Correntinos. Created on 18 September 1806, this battalion consisted of just a single company of riflemen, some 85 strong.

Granaderos Provinciales. 107 strong, this unit was commanded by Juan Florencio Terrada, a *porteno* and a former captain of Buenos Aires militia. The unit was previously called the *Granaderos de Fernando IV*.

Indios, Morenos y Pardos. This battalion was made up of the coloured inhabitants of the colony, the mulattoes, negroes and Indians. Some 352 strong, it was led by Manuel Ruiz, a captain in the old urban militia.

Marineros. Commanded by Gutierrez de la Concha, the marines were divided into six companies, with 60 men in each.

Cuerpo de Esclaves. This unit was a form of 'home guard', armed with spears and machetes.

Naturales. (Indios de Artilleria). Another unit formed from the coloured inhabitants of the colony but with a different uniform. 426 strong, the unit provided manpower for the artillery.

Arribenos. This unit comprised volunteers from the interior of the country, one grenadier and eight fusilier companies, some 435 men in all, and was commanded by Juan Pio de Gana, a Peruvian merchant who was killed in the fighting of 1807.

Artillery:

Artilleros Provinciales. Formed in October, 1806, this artillery unit was commanded by Jose Maria Pizarro. The unit was formed from the old provincial artillery.

Union de Artilleria de Buenos Aires. This artillery unit, of seven companies totalling 455 men, was formed in October, 1806, from the remains of the *Voluntarios Patriotas de la Union*, a unit created and maintained by Martin de Alzaga and afterwards by the *Cabildo*.

As explained in Chapter 3 of this book, Liniers call for volunteers went largely unanswered by many sections of the population prompting him to issue a decree of conscription, on 20 November 1806, which meant that all men between the ages of 16 and 50 were liable for military service except for the clergy, civil officials, slaves and the physically handicapped. In spite of this, however, enlistment was still not total, forcing him to issue a second decree which ordered the impressment of all those who had not yet enlisted.

In spite of the difficulties faced by Liniers, in particular from the pro-royalist groups who feared the consequences of arming the population which might one day pose a threat to Spanish rule in the colony, he did, nevertheless, establish a force of some 6,359 infantry and 1,424 cavalry. This 'New Army' as it is sometimes called, provided the nucleus of a force which, although probably no match for the British army in the field, when combined with the aggressive nature of the population of Buenos Aires, would prove to be more than a match for the British army when it made its second attempt to occupy the city in July, 1807.

In fact, following the expulsion of the British from the Rio de la Plata many of Liniers' battalions remained in existence, in some form or another, and later provided the basis for many regiments that took part in the fighting during the Wars of Liberation which raged in South America from 1808 to 1826.

Appendix V

Whitelocke's Official Report of the attack on Buenos Aires.

Copy of a letter from Lieutenant-General Whitelocke, to the Right Honourable William Wyndham, dated July 10th, 1807.

Sir,

I have the honour to acquaint you, for the information of his Majesty, that upon being joined at Monte Video, on the 15th of June, by the corps under Brigadier-General Craufurd, not one moment was lost by the Rear-Admiral and myself, in making every necessary arrangement for the attack of Buenos Ayres. After many delays, occasioned by foul winds, a landing was effected, without opposition, on the 28th of the same month, at the Ensenada de Barragon, a small bay about 30 miles to the eastward of the town. The corps employed on this expedition were, three brigades of light artillery, under Captain Frazer; the 5th, 38th, and 87th regiments of foot, under Brigadier-General Sir Samuel Auchmuty; the 17th light dragoons, 36th and 38th Regiments, under Brigadier-General the Honourable William Lumley; eight companies of the 95th regiment, and nine light infantry companies, under Brigadier-General Craufurd; four troops of the 6th dragoon guards; the 9th light dragoons; 40th and 45th regiments of foot, under Colonel the Honourable T. Mahon; all the dragoons being dismounted, except four troops of the 17th, under Lieutenant-Colonel Lloyd.

After some fatiguing marches through a country much intersected by swamps and deep muddy rivulets, the army reached Reduction, a village about nine miles distant from the bridge over the Rio Chuello, on the opposite bank of which the enemy had constructed batteries, and established a formidable line of defence. I resolved, therefore, to turn the position, by marching in two columns from my left, and crossing the river higher up, where it was represented fordable, to reunite my force in the suburbs of Buenos Ayres. I sent directions at the same time to Colonel Mahon, who was brining up the greater part of the artillery, under the protection of the 17th light dragoons, and the 40th regiment, to wait for further orders at Reduction. Major-General Levison Gower having the command of the right column, crossed the river at a pass called the Passo Chico, and falling in with a corps of the enemy, gallantly attacked and defeated it; for the particulars of which action I beg to refer you to the annex report. Owing to the ignorance of my guide, it was not until the next day that I joined with the main body of the army, when I formed my line by placing Brigadier-General Sir Samuel Auchmuty's brigade upon the left, extending it towards the convent of the Recollata, from which it was distant two miles. The 36th and 88th regiments, being on its right, Brigadier-General Craufurd's brigade occupying the central, and principal avenues of the town, being distant about three miles from the great square and fort, and the 6th dragoon guards, 9th light dragoons, and 45th regiment being his right and extending towards the Residentia. The town was thus nearly invested; and this disposition of the army, and the circumstances of the town and suburbs being divided into squares of 140 yards each side, together with the knowledge that the enemy meant to occupy the flat roofs of the houses, gave rise to the following kind of attack: – Brigadier-General Sir Samuel Auchmuty was directed to detach the 38th regiment to possess itself of the Plaza de Toros, and the adjacent strong ground and there take post. The 87th, 5th, 36th, and 88th regiments were each divided into two wings, and each wing ordered to penetrate into the street directly in its front. The light battalion divided into wings, and each followed by a wing of the 95th wing and a 3-pounder, was ordered to proceed down two streets on the right of the central one, and the 45th regiment down two adjoining, and after clearing the streets of the enemy, this latter regiment was to take post at the Residentia. Two 6-pounders were ordered along the central street, covered by the carabineers, and three troops of the 9th light dragoons, the remainder of which was posted as a reserve in the centre. Each division was ordered to proceed along the street directly in its front, till it arrived at the last square of houses next the river Plata, of which it was to possess itself, forming on the flat roofs, and there wait for further orders. The 95th regiment was to occupy two of the most commanding situations from which it could annoy the enemy. Two corporals, with tools, were ordered to march at the head of each column, for the purpose of breaking open the doors. The whole were unloaded, and no firing was to be permitted until the columns had reached their final points, and formed. A cannonade in the central streets was the signal for the whole to move forward.

In conformity of this arrangement, at half-past six o'clock of the morning of the 5th instant, the 38th regiment moving towards its left, and the 87th straight to its front, approached the strong post of the Retiro and Plaza de Toros; and, after a most vigorous and spirited attack, in which these regiments suffered much from grape-shot and musketry, their gallant commander, Brigadier-General Sir Samuel Auchmuty, possessed himself of the post, taking 32 pieces of cannon, an immense quantity of ammunition, and 600 prisoners. The 5th regiment, meeting with but little opposition, proceeded to the river, and took possession of the church and convent of Saint Catalina. The 36th and 88th regiments, under Brigadier-General Lumley, moving in the appointed order, were soon opposed by a heavy and continued fire of musketry from the tops and windows of the houses, the doors of which were barricaded in so strong a manner, as to render them almost impossible to force: the streets were intersected by deep ditches, on the inside of which were planted cannon, pouring showers of grape on the advancing columns. In defiance, however, of this opposition, the 36th regiment, headed by the gallant General, reached its final destination; but the 88th, being nearer to the fort and principal defences of the enemy, were so weakened by his fire, as to be totally overpowered and taken. The flank of the 36th being thus exposed, this regiment, together with the 5th, retired upon Sir Samuel Auchmuty's post, at the Plaza de Toros, not, however, before Lieutenant-Colonel Burne, and the grenadier company of the 36th regiment, had an opportunity of distinguishing themselves, by charging about 500 of the enemy, and taking and spiking two guns. The two 6-pounders moving up the central streets, meeting with a very superior fire, the four troops of the carabineers, led on by Lieutenant-Colonel Kington, advanced to take the battery opposed to them; but this gallant officer being unfortunately wounded, as well as Captain Burrell, next in command, and the fire, both from the battery and houses, proving very destructive, they retreated to a short distance, but continued to occupy a position in front of the enemy's principal defences, and considerably in advance of that which they had taken in the morning.

The left division of Brigadier-General Craufurd's brigade, under Lieutenant-Colonel Pack, passed on nearly to the river, and, turning to the left, approached the great square, with the intention of possessing itself of the Jesuits' College, a situation which commanded the enemy's principal line of defence; but, from the very destructive nature of his fire, this was found impracticable; and after sustaining a heavy loss, one part of the division throwing itself into a house, which was afterwards not found tenable, was shortly obliged to surrender, whilst the remaining part, after enduring a dreadful fire with the greatest intrepidity, Lieutenant-Colonel Pack, its commander, being wounded, retired upon the right division, commanded by Brigadier-General Craufurd himself. This division having passed quite through to the river Plate, turned also to the left, to approach the great square and fort, from the north-east bastion of which it was distant about 400 yards, when Brigadier-General Craufurd, learning the fate of his left division, thought it most advisable to take possession of the convent of Saint Domingo, near which he then was, intending to proceed onwards to the Franciscan church, which lay still nearer the fort, if the attack or success of any other of our columns should free him, in some measure, from the host of enemies which surrounded him. The 45th regiment, being further from the enemy's centre, had gained the Residentia without much opposition; and Lieutenant-Colonel Guard, leaving it in possession of his battalion companies, moved down with the grenadier company towards the centre of the town, and joined Brigadier-General Craufurd. The enemy, who now surrounded the convent on all sides, attempting to take a 3-pounder which lay in the street, the Lieutenant-Colonel with his company and a few light infantry under Major Trotter, charged them with great spirit; in an instant the greater part of his company and Major Trotter were killed, but the gun was saved. The Brigadier-General was now obliged to confine himself to the defence of the convent, from which the rifleman kept up a well-directed fire upon such of the enemy as approached the post; but the quantity of round shot, grape, and musketry, to which they were exposed, at last obliged them to quit the top of the building; and the enemy, to the number of 6,000, bringing up cannon to force the wooden gates which fronted the fort, the Brigadier-General having no communication with any other columns, and judging from the cessation of firing that those next him had not been successful, surrendered at four o'clock in the afternoon. The result of this day's action had left me in possession of the Plaza de Toros, a strong post on the enemy's right, and the Residentia, another strong post on his left, whilst I occupied an advanced position opposite his centre. But these advantages had cost about 2,500 men in killed, wounded, and prisoners. The nature of the fire to which the troops were exposed was violent in the extreme. Grape-shot at the corners of all streets, musketry, hand-grenades, bricks and stones from the tops of all the houses. Every householder, with his negroes, defended his dwelling, each of which was in itself a fortress; and it is perhaps not too much to say, that the whole male population of Buenos Ayres was employed in its defence. This was the situation of the army on the morning of the 6th instant, when General Liniers addressed a letter to me, offering to give up all his prisoners taken in the late affair, together with the 71st regiment, and others taken with Brigadier-General Beresford, if I desisted from any further attack on the town, and withdraw his Majesty's forces from the river Plata; intimating at the same time, that from the exasperated state of the populace, he could not answer for the safety of the prisoners, if I persisted in offensive measures. Influenced by this consideration (which I

146

knew, from better authority, to be founded in fact), and reflecting of how little advantage would be the possession of a country, the inhabitants of which were so absolutely hostile, I resolved to forego the advantages which the bravery of the troops had obtained, and accede to the annexed treaty, which I trust will meet the approbation of his Majesty.

I have nothing further to add, except to mention, in terms of the highest praise, the conduct of Rear-Admiral Murray, whose cordial co-operation has never been wanting whenever the army could be benefited by his exertions. Captain Rowley, of the royal navy, commanding the seamen on shore; Captain Bayntun, of his Majesty's ship Africa, who superintended the disembarkation; and Captain Thomson, of the Fly, who had the direction of the gun-boats, and had previously rendered me much service, by reconnoitring the river, are all entitled to my best thanks.

As his character already stands so high, it is almost unnecessary to state, that from my second-in-command, Major-General Levison Gower, I have experienced every zealous and useful assistance. My thanks are likewise due to Brigadier-Generals Sir Samuel Auchmuty and Lumley, and to Colonel Mahon, and to Brigadier-General Craufurd, commanding brigades. I cannot sufficiently bring to notice the uncommon exertions of Captain Frazer, commanding the royal artillery, the fertility of whose mind, zeal and animation in all cases, left difficulties behind. Captain Squire, of the royal engineers, is also entitled to my best thanks. Nor should I omit the gallant conduct of Major Nichols, of the 45th regiment, who, on the morning of the 6th instant, being pressed by the enemy, near the Residentia, charged them with great spirit, and took two howitzers and many prisoners. Lieutenant-Colonel Bradford, Deputy Adjutant-General, has likewise a great claim to my approbation, as a gallant and promising officer. The officers of my personal staff, Lieutenant-Colonel Torrens, Military Secretary, Captains Brown, Foster, Douglas, and Whittingham, Aides-de-Camp, must also be mentioned by me in terms of just regard. The knowledge which the latter possesses of the Spanish language has been eminently useful to me.

This despatch will be delivered to you by Lieutenant-Colonel Bourke, Deputy-Quarter-Master-General, who has afforded me that assistance which might be looked for from an officer of his military talents and attachment to the service; to whom I beg to refer you for any further particulars respecting the military operations in this part of the world.

I have the honour to be, &c.

JOHN WHITELOCKE,
Lieutenant-General.

Endnotes

CHAPTER 1

1. Hon. J. W. Fortescue, *The History of the British Army*, (London, 1921), v. 313.
2. Theodore Hood, *The Life of General the Honourable Sir David Baird, Bart*, (London, 1833), 139–140.
3. Popham, in Hood, *Sir David Baird*, 142–148.
4. From a census taken in 1806. Ernestina Costa, *English Invasion of the River Plate*, (Buenos Aires, 1937), 30.

CHAPTER 2

1. Ernestina Costa, *English Invasion of the River Plate*, (Buenos Aires, 1937), 31.
2. Maj. Alexander Gillespie, *Gleanings and Remarks; collected during many months of Residence at Buenos Aires, and within the Upper Country.* (Leeds, 1818), 43.
3. Ibid. 46–47.
4. Thomas Fernyhough, *Military Memoirs of Four Brothers (Natives of Staffordshire) engaged in the service of their country as well as in the New World and Africa, as on the Continent of Europe. By the Survivor*, (London, 1829), 92.
5. Costa, *English Invasion*, 38.
6. William Gavin, in *The Diary of William Gavin*, in 'The Highland Light Infantry Chronicle', (Glasgow, 1899), 5.
7. Beresford, in Costa, *English Invasion*, 40.
8. Gillespie, *Gleanings and Remarks*, 50.

9. Beresford, in Costa, *English Invasion*, 42–43.

10. Gavin, *Diary*, 5.

11. Gillespie, *Gleanings and Remarks*, 52.

12. Ibid, 53.

13. Thomas Pococke, *Journal of Captain Pococke*, in 'The Highland Light Infantry Chronicle', (Glasgow, 1899), 193.

14. Beresford, in Costa, *English Invasion*, 50.

15. Pococke, *Journal*, 195.

16. Ibid. 195.

17. Ibid. 195.

CHAPTER THREE

1. Popham, quoted in Ernestina Costa, *English Invasion of the River Plate*, (Buenos Aires, 1937), 54.

2. Pococke, *Journal of Thomas Pococke*, in 'The Highland Light Infantry Chronicle', (Glasgow, 1899), 21.

3. Thomas Fernyhough, *Military Memoirs of Four Brothers (Natives of Staffs) engaged in the service of their country, as well as in the New World and Africa, as on the Continent of Europe. By the Survivor*, (London, 1829), 98.

4. Pococke, *Journal*, 211.

5. Beresford, in Costa, *English Invasion*, 58.

6. Fernyhough, *Military Memoirs*, 99.

7. Pococke, *Journal*, 213.

8. Fernyhough, *Military Memoirs*, 100.

9. Pococke, *Journal*, 214.

10. Ibid. 214.

11. Fernyhough, *Military Memoirs*, 101.

12. Ibid. 101. British casualties had been 165 killed, wounded and missing. The Hon. J. W. Fortescue, *History of the British Army*, (London, 1921), v, 370.

13. Beresford, in Costa, *English Invasion*, 64.

14. Costa, ibid. 67.

15. Beresford, ibid, 68–70.

16. Sobremonte, ibid, 82–83.

CHAPTER FOUR

1. Backhouse, in *The European Magazine*, (London, 1807), li, 145–146.

2. Hon. J. W. Fortescue, *History of the British Army*, (London, 1921), v, 375.

3. Ibid. v, 377.
4. Christopher Hibbert, *A Soldier of the 71st*, (London, 1975), 1.
5. Lawrence, *The Autobiography of Sgt. William Lawrence, a hero of the Peninsular and Waterloo Campaigns*, (London, 1881), 20–21.
6. Ibid. 21.
7. Ernestina Costa, *English Invasion of the River Plate*, (Buenos Aires, 1937), 82–83.
8. Hibbert, *Soldier of the 71st*, 2.
9. Lawrence, *Autobiography*, 23.
10. Hibbert, *Soldier of the 71st*, 2–3.
11. Lawrence, *Autobiography*, 23.
12. Maj. A. Tucker, *Narrative of the Operations of a small British Force, under the Command of Brigadier-General Sir Samuel Auchmuty, employed in the reduction of Montevideo on the River Plate. A.D. 1807. By a field officer of the staff*, (London, 1807), 12.
13. Lawrence, *Autobiography*, 23.
14. Hibbert, *Soldier of the 71st*, 3.
15. Lawrence, *Autobiography*, 24.
16. Harry Smith, *The Autobiography of Sir Harry Smith, Baronet of Aliwal on the Sutlej, GCB*, (London, 1902), 5.
17. Lawrence, *Autobiography*, 25.
18. J. W. Williams, *History of the Argentine Republic, Vol. 1. 1492–1807*, *translated from the Spanish by J. W. Williams*, (Buenos Aires, 1865), 132.
19. Ibid. 133.

CHAPTER FIVE

1. Pococke, *Journal of Thomas Pococke*, in 'The Highland Light Infantry Chronicle', (Glasgow, 1899), 531.
2. Ibid. 475.
3. Ibid. 475.
4. Beresford, quoted in Ernestina Costa, *English Invasion of the River Plate*, (Buenos Aires, 1937), 76–77.
5. Hon. J. W. Fortescue, *History of the British Army*, (London, 1921), v. 387–388.
6. William Lawrence, *The Autobiography of Sgt. William Lawrence, a hero of the Peninsular and Waterloo Campaigns*, (London, 1881), 26–27.
7. Ibid. 27–28.
8. Whitelocke, in Costa, *English Invasion*, 94.
9. Lawrence, *Autobiography*, 29–30.
10. Harry Smith, *The Autobiography of Sir Harry Smith, Baronet of Aliwal on the Sutlej, GCB*, (London, 1902), 6.
11. Christopher Hibbert, *A Soldier of the 71st*, (London, 1975), 7.

12. Lumley, in Blanchard and Ramsey, *Trial at Large of Lt. Gen. Whitelocke, Late Commander-in-Chief of the Forces in South America, by America, by General Court Martial, Held at Chelsea Hospital on Thursday, January 28th, 1808*, (London, 1808), 159.
13. Ibid. 160.
14. Lawrence, *Autobiography*, 31.
15. Ibid. 32.
16. Ibid. 32.
17. Craufurd, in *Trial at Large*, 116.
18. Bourke, in *Trial at Large*, 63.
19. Gower, in *Trial at Large*, 13.

CHAPTER SIX

1. Bourke, in Blanchard and Ramsey, *The Trial at Large of Lieut-General Whitelocke, Lat Commander-in-Chief of the Forces in South America, by General Court Martial, Held at Chelsea Hospital on Thursday, January 28th, 1808*, (London, 1808), 65.
2. Christopher Hibbert, *A Soldier of the 71st*, (London, 1975), 8.
3. Anon, *A Narrative of the Expedition to and the Storming of Buenos Aires, by the British Army, Commanded by Lieutenant-General Whitelocke. By an Officer attached to the Expedition*, (Bath, 1807), 6–7.
4. Anon, *An Authentic Narrative of the Proceedings of the Expedition under the Command of Brigadier-General Craufurd, Until its arrival at Monte Video, with an account of the Operations against Buenos Aires under the command of Lieutenant-General Whitelocke. By an Officer of the Expedition*, (London, 1808), 126.
5. Craufurd, in Ernestina Costa, *English Invasion of the River Plate*, (Buenos Aires, 1937), 260–261.
6. Holland, in Col. Willoughby Verner's *History and Campaigns of the Rifle Brigade*, (London, 1912), i, 104.
7. Anon, *An Authentic Narrative*, 129.
8. Craufurd, in *Trial at Large*, 124–125.
9. Ibid. 125.
10. Liniers, in Costa, *English Invasion*, 106.
11. Craufurd, in *Trial at Large*, 125–126.
12. E. W. Sheppard, *The Ninth Queen's Royal Lancers, 1715–1936*, (Aldershot, 1938), 58.
13. Anon, *A Narrative*, 10.
14. Whitelocke, in Costa, *English Invasion*, 113.
15. Nicholls, in Col. H. C. Wylly's *History of the 1st and 2nd Battalions The Sherwood Foresters, Nottingham and Derbyshire Regiment, 1790–1914*,

(London, 1929), 119.

16. Stephen Morley, *Memoirs of a Sergeant of the 5th Regiment of Foot*, (London, 1842), 30.

17. Anon, *A Narrative*, 10–11.

18. Roche, in Costa, *English Invasion*, 111.

19. United Services Magazine, *Minor Expeditions of the British Army, 1803–1815*, (London, 1905–06).

20. Liniers, in Costa, *English Invasion*, 117–118.

CHAPTER SEVEN

1. Ernestina Costa, *English Invasion of the River Plate*, (Buenos Aires, 1937), 126.

2. Ibid. 126.

3. Stephen Morley, *Memoirs of a Sergeant of the 5th Regiment of Foot*, (London 1842), 35.

4. Anon, *A Narrative of the Expedition to and the Storming of Buenos Aires, by the British Army, Commanded by Lieutenant-General Whitelocke. By an Officer attached to the Expedition*, (Bath, 1807), 23.

5. Christopher Hibbert, *Soldier of the 71st*, (London, 1975), 8–9.

6. Craufurd, in *Trial at Large of Lieut. General Whitelocke, Late Commander-in-Chief of the Forces in South America, by General Court Martial, Held at Chelsea Hospital, on Thursday, January 28th, 1808*, (London, 1808), 382.

7. Hibbert, *Soldier of the 71st*, 9.

8. Craufurd, in *Trial at Large*, 384.

9. Morley, *Memoirs of a Sergeant*, 35–36.

CHAPTER EIGHT

1. Whittingham, Maj-Gen. F., *A Memoir of the Services of Lieutenant-General Sir Samuel Ford Whittingham, KCB, KCH, GCF*, (London, 1868), 322.

2. Nicholls, in Col. H. C. Wylly's *History of the 1st and 2nd Battalions The Sherwood Foresters, Nottinghamshire and Derbyshire Regiments, 1790–1914*, (London, 1929), 125.

3. Alzaga, in Ernestina Costa's *English Invasion of the River Plate*, (Buenos Aires, 1937), 148.

4. Whitelocke, in Costa, *English Invasion*, 150–151.

5. Nicholls, in Wylly, *Sherwood Foresters*, 125–126.

6. Whitelocke, in Costa, *English Invasion*, 154–155.

7. Ibid. 155–156.

8. Anon. *A Narrative of the Expedition to and Storming of Buenos Aires, by the British Army*. (Bath, 1807), 31.

9. Fraser, in Costa, *English Invasion*, 157.

10. Harry Smith, *The Autobiography of Sir Harry Smith, Baronet of Aliwal on the Sutlej, GCB*, (London, 1902), 10.

11. Christopher Hibbert, *A Soldier of the 71st*, (London, 1975), 10.

12. Tom Plunkett in *The United Services Magazine*, (London, 1842), 69.

13. Costa, *English Invasion*, 158.

14. Whittingham, *A Memoir of the Services*, 23–24.

CHAPTER NINE

1. J.W. Fortescue, *History of the British Army*, (London, 1921), v, 432.

2. Ibid. 431.

3. Blanchard and Ramsey, *The Trial at Large of Lieutenant-General Whitelocke, Late Commander-in-Chief of the Forces in South-America, by General Court Martial, Held at Chelsea Hospital, on Thursday, January 28th, 1808*, (London, 1808). (Sentence) 3.

4. United Services Magazine, *Minor Expeditions of the British Army, 1803–1815*, (London, 1905–06), 513.

5. J.W. Williams, *Dominguez' 'History of the Argentine Republic, 1492–1807,' Translated from the Spanish by J.W. Williams*, (Buenos Aires, 1865), i, 148.

Bibliography

Alzaga, Enrique Williams. *Fuga del General Beresford*. Buenos Aires, 1965.

Anon. A *Narrative of the Expedition to and the Storming of Buenos Aires, by the British Army, Commanded by Lieutenant-General Whitelocke. By an Officer attached to the Expedition*. Bath, 1807.

Anon. *An Authentic Narrative of the Proceedings of the Expedition under the Command of Brigadier-General Craufurd, Until its arrival at Monte Video, with an account of the Operations against Buenos Aires under the Command of Lieutenant-General Whitelocke. By an Officer of the Expedition*. London, 1808.

Anon. *Authentic Narrative of the Proceedings of the Expedition against Buenos Aires. By an Irish Officer*. Dublin, 1808.

Anon. *Truth and Reason, versus Calumny and Folly; In which the leading Circumstances of General Whitelocke conduct in South America are Examined*. London, 1808.

Beverina, Juan. *Las Invasiones Inglesas al Rio de la Plata, 1806–1807*. Buenos Aires, 1937.

Blanchard and Ramsey. *The Trial at Large of Lieut-Gen. Whitelocke, Late Commander-in-Chief of the Forces in South America, by General Court Martial, Held at Chelsea Hospital on Thursday, January 28th, 1808*. London, 1808.

Campbell, Leon G. *The Military and Society in Colonial Peru, 1750–1810*. Philadelphia, 1978.

Capdevila, Arturo. *Las Invasiones Inglesas, Cronica y Evocation*. Buenos Aires, 1938.

Compton, Herbert. *A Master Mariner. Being the Life and Adventures of Captain Robert William Eastwick*. London, 1891.

Corbellini, Enrique C. *La Revolucion de Mayo y sus antecedentes desde las invasiones inglesas*. Buenos Aires, 1950.

Costa, Ernestina. *English Invasion of the Rio de la Plata*. Buenos Aires, 1937.

Craufurd, Alexander H. *General Craufurd and his Light Division, with many anecdotes, a paper and letters by Sir John Moore, and also letters from the Rt. Hon. W. Windham, the Duke of Wellington, and others*. London, 1891.

Cronica General Del Uruguay. *Las Invasiones Inglesas*. Vol.2, No.1. Montevideo. n.d.

Cunliffe, Marcus. *The Royal Irish Fusiliers, 1 793-1950*. London, 1952.

Dalton, Maj-Gen. J.C. *Buenos Aires and Montevideo, 1806 and 1807*. Journal of the Royal Artillery, Vol.54. Woolwich, 1926-27.

Destefani, Laurio H. *Los Marinos en Las Invasiones Inglesas*. Buenos Aires, 1975.

Fernyhough, Thomas. *Military Memoirs of Four Brothers (Natives of Staffordshire) engaged in the service of their country, as well as in the New World and Africa, as on the Continent of Europe. By the Survivor*. London, 1829.

Fortescue, The Hon. J.W. *The History of the British Army*. London, Vol.5, 1921.

Fortin, Jorge L.R. *Invasiones Inglesas*. Buenos Aires, 1967.

Gillespie, Maj. Alexander. *Gleanings and remarks; collected during many months of Residence at Buenos Aires, and within the Upper Country*. Leeds, 1818.

Groussac, Paul. *Santiago Liniers, Conde de Buenos Aires, 1753-1810*. Buenos Aires, 1907.

Hibbert, Christopher. *A Soldier of the 71st*. London, 1975.

The Highland Light Infantry Chronicle. *British Invasions of the Rio de la Plata*. Glasgow, Vol.8, 1939.

————————*Diary of William Gavin*. Glasgow, 1899.

————————*Journal of Captain Pococke*. Glasgow, 1899.

Hood, Theodore. *The Life of General the Right Honourable Sir David Baird, Bart*. London, 1833.

Iconographica. *Iconographica de los Uniformes Militaires, Invasiones Inglesas, 1807*. Buenos Aires, 1967.

Jones, James P. *A History of the South Staffordshire Regiment, 1705–1923*. Wolverhampton, 1923.

Kalendario. *Kalendario Manual y Guia de Forasteros en Madrid para el Ano de 1806*. Madrid, 1806.

Lawrence, William. *The Autobiography of Sgt. William Lawrence, a hero of the Peninsular and Waterloo Campaigns*. London, 1881.

Levene, Ricardo. *Lecciones de Historia Argentina*. Buenos Aires, 1917

Lopez, Manuel Castro. *El Tercio de Gailcia en Las Defensa de Buenos Aires*. Buenos Aires, 1911.

Lynch, John. *Spanish Colonial Administration, 1782–1810. The Intendant System in the Viceroyalty of the Rio de la Plata.* London, 1958.

Morley, Stephen. *Memoirs of a Sergeant of the 5th Regiment of Foot.* London, 1842.

Mulhall, Michael. *The English in South America.* London, 1877.

Mullaly, Col. B.R. *The South Lancashire Regiment, The Prince of Wales's Volunteers.* Bristol, 1955.

Oatts, Lt-Col. L.B. Proud Heritage. *The Story of the Highland Light Infantry. Vol.1.* London, 1953.

Pearson, Isaac R. *Narraciones historicas americanas. Las invasiones inglesas.* Buenos Aires, 1901.

Pereira, Antonio N. *La Invasion inglesa al Rio de la Plata.* Montevideo, 1877.

Popham, Sir Home. *Minutes of a Court Martial, Held on board His Majesty's Ship Gladiator, in Portsmouth Harbour, On Friday, the 6th day of March, 1807.* London, 1807.

Puentes, Gabriel A. *Don Francisco Javier de Elio en el Rio de la Plata.* Buenos Aires, 1966.

Reconquista y Defensa. *La Reconquista y Defensa de Buenos Aires. Publicacion del Instituto de Estudios Historicos sobre la Reconquista y Defensa de Buenos Aires, 1806–1807.* Buenos Aires, 1947.

Revista Militar. *La Historia Patria y la Accion de Sus Armas. Publicacion Especial del Circulo Militar Argentino. Vols, 186–188.* Buenos Aires, 1960.

Roberts, Carlos. *Las Invasiones Inglesas del Rio de la Plata (1806–1807) Y la Influencia Inglesa en la Independencia y Organizacion de las Provincias del Rio de la Plata.* Buenos Aires, 1938.

Robertson, William F. *The Life of Miranda,* London, 1929.

Royal Military Calendar. *Royal Military Calendar or Army Service and Commission Book. Vol.3.* London, 1820.

Sagui, Francisco. *Los ultimos cuatro anos de la dominacion espanola en la antiguo Virreinato del Rio de la Plata desde 26 de junio 1806 hasta 25 de mayo 1810.* Buenos Aires, 1874.

Salas, Alberto M. *Diario de Buenos Aires, 1806–1807.* Buenos Aires, 1981.

Sanchez, Ramos, Ignacio. *En el Virreinato del Rio de la Plata. Don Rafael de Sobremonte. Secretario de Vertiz; Gobernado Intendente de Cordoba; Inspector de Armas; Virrey; Mariscal de Campo; Consejero de Indias.* Buenos Aires, 1929.

Sheppard, Maj. E.W. *The Ninth Queen's Royal Lancers, 1715–1936.* Aldershot, 1938.

Smith, Harry. *The Autobiography of Sir Harry Smith, Baronet of Aliwal on the Sutlej, GCB.* London, 1902.

Tucker, Maj. A. *Narrative of the Operations of a small British Force, under the Command of Brigadier-General Sir Samuel Auchmuty, employed in the reduction of Montevideo on the Rio de la Plata. A.D. 1807. By a field officer of the staff.* London, 1807.

The Southern Star. *The Southern Star, or Estella del Sur. (Facsimile)* Montevideo, 1942.

United Services Magazine. *Minor Expeditions of the British Army, 1803–1815.* London, 1905–1906.

——————————*Rifleman Tom Plunkett.* London, 1842.

Verner, Col. Willoughby. *History and Campaigns of the Rifle Brigade.* London, 1912.

Vidal, E.E. *Picturesque Illustrations of Buenos Aires and Montevideo.* London, 1820.

Walker, H.M. *A History of the Northumberland Fusiliers, 1674–1902.* London, 1929.

Whittingham, Maj-Gen. F. *A Memoir of the Services of Lieutenant-General Sir Samuel Ford Whittingham, KCB, KCH, GCF.* London, 1868.

Williams, J.W. Dominguez' *'History of the Argentine Republic'. Vol.1, 1492–1807. Translated from the Spanish by J. W. Williams.* Buenos Aires, 1865.

Wylly, Col. H. C. *History of the 1st and 2nd Battalions The Sherwood Foresters, Nottinghamshire and Derbyshire Regiment, 1790–1914.* 1929.

Map Section

Provinces of the Rio de la Plata

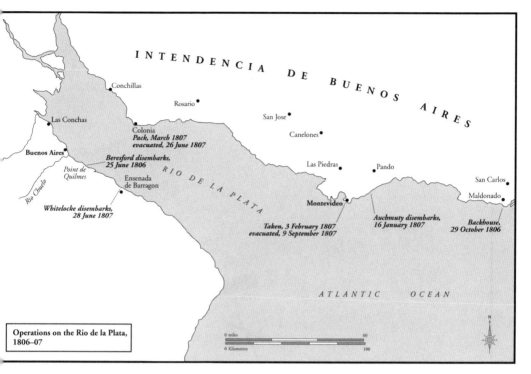

Operations in the Rio de la Plata

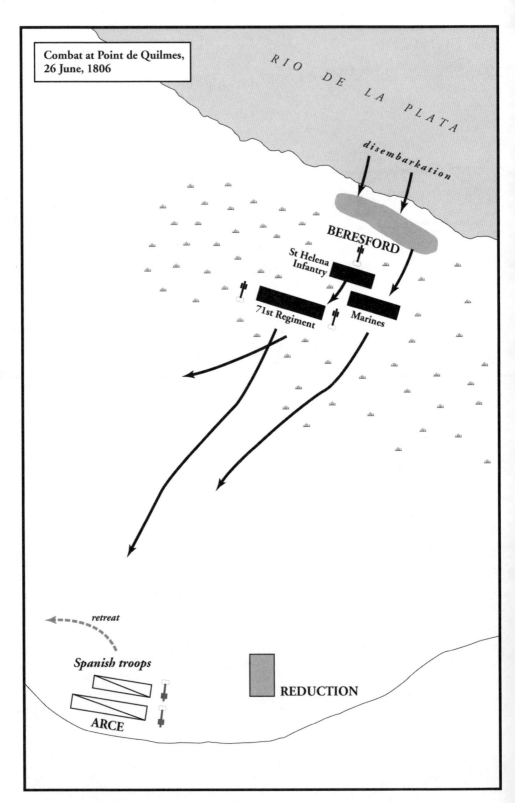

Combat at Point de Quilmes, 26 June 1806

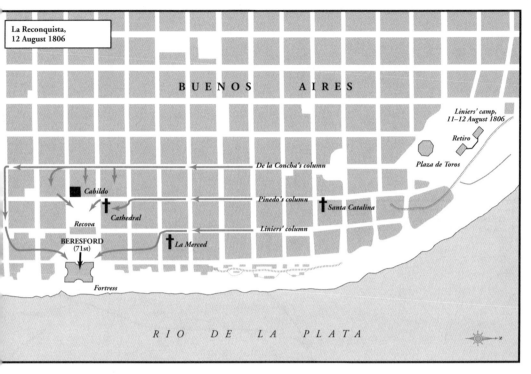

La Reconquista: Liniers' attack, 12 August 1806

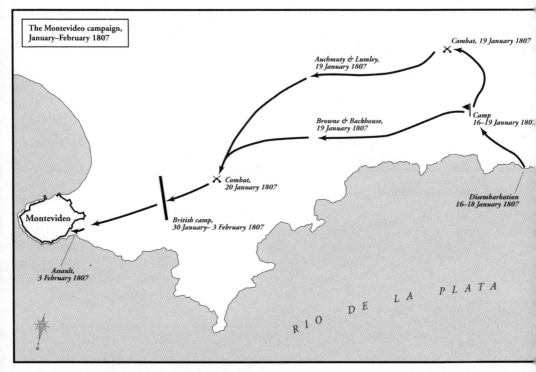

The Montevideo Campaign, Jan/Feb 1807

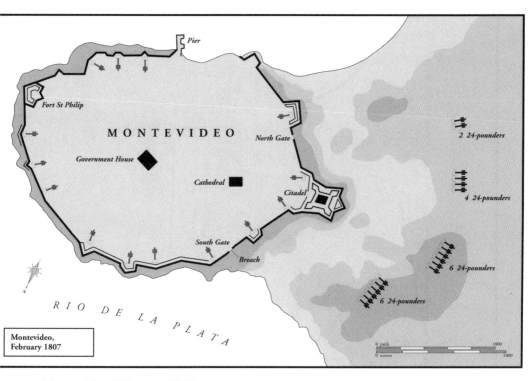

Montevideo, February 1807

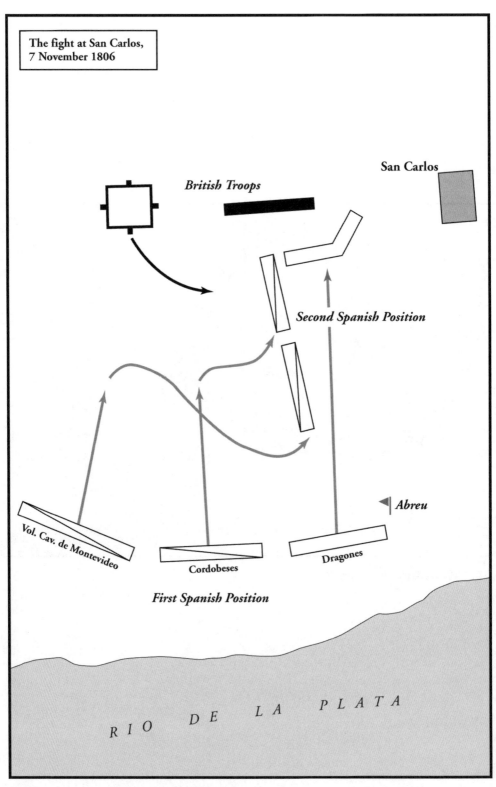

The Fight at San Carlos, 7 November 1806

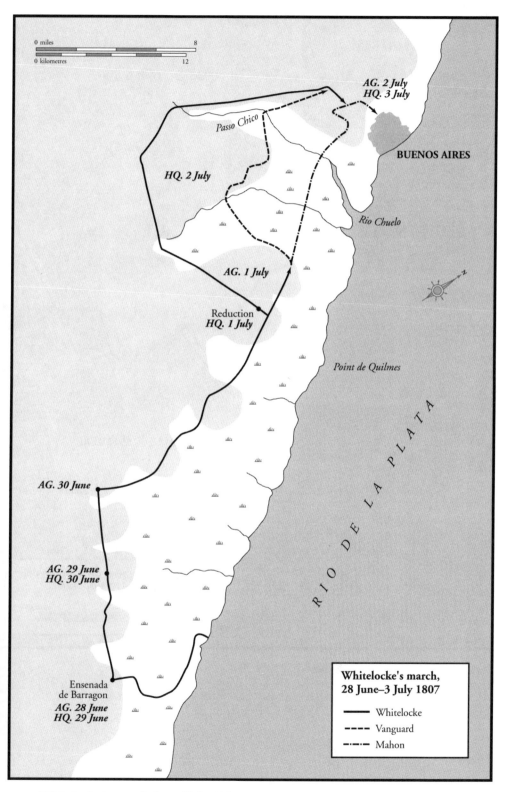

Whitelocke's march, June/July 1807

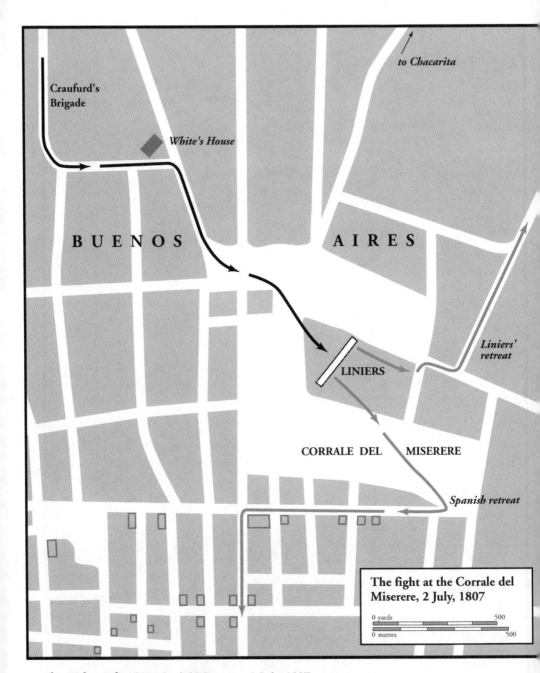

The Fight at the Corrale del Miserere, 2 July 1807

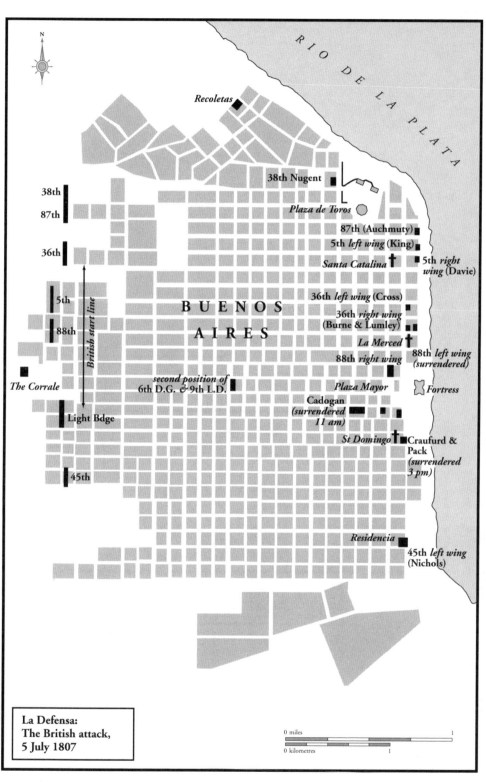

La Defensa: The British attack, 5 July 1807

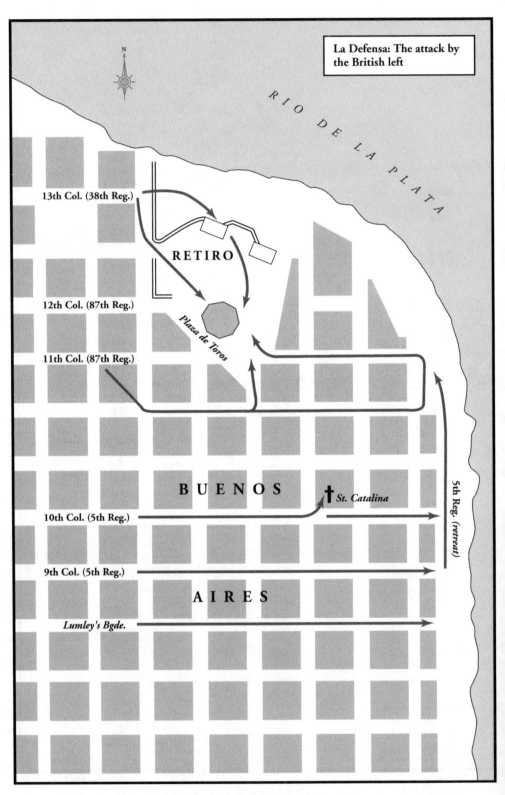

La Defensa: The attack by the British left

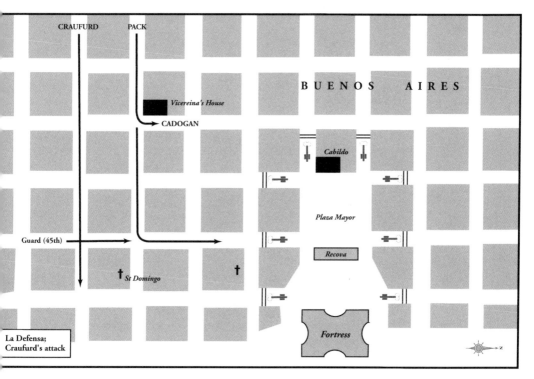

La Defensa: Craufurd's attack

Index

Abercromby, Sir Ralph, xii, 5, 42
Abreu, Augustin, 44
Addington, Lord, 2
Allende, Colonel, 51
Alte Gracia, 38
Alzaga, Martin de, 21, 437, 58, 63, 86-7. 114-15, 119
Arbuthnot, Captain, 17, 22, 37
Arce, Pedro, 15, 40, 55
Auchmuty, Brig-Gen. Sir Samuel, xxii, 5, 19, 42-3, 47-59, 61, 64-8, 73, 80, 85, 90-1, 93-4, 97, 99-100, 103-4, 110-11, 115-16, 128, 143-5, 147
Backhouse, Lt. Col. 19, 42-4, 48, 50, 71
Badajoz, siege of, 98, 129
Baird, Sir David, xi-xiii, 4-5, 18-19, 42-3
Balbiani, Caser, 81, 86-7
Beresford, Brig-Gen. William Carr, 4-7, 9, 13-19, 21-3, 25-39, 41-3, 46-7, 53, 61-4, 72, 76, 80, 90-1, 108, 114-15, 117, 122, 125, 127-29, 139, 146
Blauberg, battle at, xiii
Bolivar, Simon, 128-9
Bone, Surgeon, 96

Bourke, Lt. Col. Richard, 49, 72, 76, 80, 147
Bradford, Lt. Col. Thomas, 115, 147
Browne, Col. 49-50, 52, 56, 73
Brownrigg, Sir Robert, 51, 65, 58, 64
Buceo, 49
Buenos Aires, 3, 7, 8-9, 11-23, 25-30, 35-6, 38-9, 41-53, 55-9, 61-68, 71-3, 75-82, 84, 86-93, 100, 103-4, 107, 109, 112, 114-130, 135-6, 139-43
Burne, Lt. Col. 100, 145
Burrell, Capt. 110, 145
Butler, Lt. Col. Sir Edward, 94
Cacerios de Perdriel, 21
Cadogan, Lt. Col. Henry, 105-6, 111, 127
Calamuchita Valley, 62
Cape Colony, xiii, 4-5, 19-20, 39
Cape de Verde, 47
Cape of Good Hope, xi-xii, 42, 47
Cape St. Mary, 8
Cape Town, xiii, 5
Capilla, 39
Casamayor, Felix, 35
Catamarca, 63

Cathcart, Lt.Gen. 123
Cespedes, Martina, 120
Chain, Benito, 26
Chawner, Lieut. 49
Ciudad Rodrigo, siege of, 127, 129
Colonia, 25-7, 55, 58, 67, 69-70, 72-4
Concha, Gutierrez de la, 30-32, 34, 81, 86-8, 94, 97, 141
Conchillas, 55
Connelans, 68-70
Cordoba, 16, 38, 51, 127-8
Corrale del Miserere, 82-3, 85-7, 89, 91, 106, 110, 113, 114-15, 124
Cornwallis, Lord, 2, 45
Corunna, 128
Craufurd, Brig-Gen. Robert, 45-8, 64, 68-9, 71-3, 75, 78, 81-4, 90, 104, 106-9, 111, 113-14, 121, 124-5, 127, 137, 143-7
Cuesta, General, 129
Cuyo, 128
Davie, Lt. Col. Humphrey, 94, 97, 99, 111
Donnelly, Captain, 42, 52
Duff, Lt. Col. Alexander, 102-3, 108, 111, 136
Dundas, Lt. Gen. David, 123
Elio, General, 69-70, 81-2, 86, 88-9, 129
Ensenada de Barragon, 25, 28, 64, 72, 74-8, 124, 135, 143
'Estella del Sur', 66
Everard, Lieut. 56
Fernyhough, Robert, 14, 29, 31, 33-4
Fraser, Capt. Augustus S, 118
Garcia, Captain Pedro Manuel, 26
Gardiner, Major, 56, 70
Gavin, Ensign William, 15, 19
Gillespie, Maj. Alexander, 13-14, 17, 20-1, 62
Gordon, Colonel, 5
Goretti, island of, 43, 48

Gower, Maj-Gen, Leveson, 65-6, 73-6, 78-85, 88-90, 102, 106, 110, 115-19, 124-5, 127, 135, 144, 147
Grenville, Lord, 1, 4, 46
Guard, Lt. Col. 104, 106-11, 146
Guemes, Martin, 52
Hood, Lord, 5
Hotham, Vice-Admiral, 5
Huidobro, Ruis, 25-6, 50-1, 55-6, 128
Huiz, Fransisco, 44
Hyder Ali, xi, xiii, 42
Ironmonger, Maj. 102
Janssen, General, xiii
Kennet, Captain, 31
King, Maj. Henry, 95-9, 111
King George III, xii, 18
Kington, Lt. Col. 109-10, 145
La Chacarita, 83, 87
Lake, Lt. Gen. 123
Las Conchas, 25-7
Las Palmas, 27
Las Piedras, 55
Lawrence, Sgt. William, 53, 65, 67, 69-70, 78
Lecocq, Bernado, 52
L'Espados, 68
Liniers, Santiago, 25-40, 55-6, 63, 78, 80-83, 86-90, 108, 114-121, 127-29, 139-142, 146,
Los Condones, 62
Lloyd, Lt. Col. Ewan, 78, 143
Lujan, 16-17, 39, 63
Lumley, Brig. Gen. William, 49-50, 68-9, 73, 78-82, 84, 98, 100-101, 103-4, 111, 142, 145, 147
Luxton, Sergeant William, 57
Mahon, Col. Thomas, 71, 73, 79, 80-1, 86, 88, 113, 115, 142, 144, 147
Maldonado, 43-4, 48
Marsden, Sir William, 7
Martinez, Captain, 44, 62
Meadows, Gen. Sir William, 123

Medina del Rio Seco, battle of, 129
Melville, Lord, 3-4, 7
Mendoza, 38, 128
Merle, Colonel Ignacio, 16, 129
Miranda, Francisco de, 1-4, 128
Montevideo, 8-9, 12, 24, 26, 38, 40-59 passim, 61-9, 71-3, 90, 114-15, 117-19, 121-24, 128-9, 136
Moore, Lt. Gen. Sir John, 123, 127
Mordeile, Hipolito, 34
Moreno, 43-44
Morley, Stephen, 85, 99
Mulgrave, Lord, 5
Munro, Sir Hector, xi
Murray, Rear-Admiral, 47-8, 71, 119, 147
Murray, George, 5
Napoleon, 1, 19, 126
Nicholls, (Major) Lt. Col. Jasper, 104, 107, 111, 113-114
Nugent, Lt. Col. John, 56, 97-8
Orinocco River, 3
Pack, Lt. Col. Denis, 4, 29, 35, 39, 62-4, 67, 69-70, 72, 74, 90, 104-9, 111, 118-19, 124, 127-8, 145
Padilla, Aniceto, 63, 66
Passo Chico, 80-82, 85
Peninsular War, xiii, 4, 45, 99, 109, 127-9
Perdriel, 21, 25-6
Pina, Saturnino Rodriguez, 63, 66
Pinedo, Colonel, 30-31
Pitt, William, xi, 1-4, 7
Pococke, Captain Thomas, 21-3, 27, 29, 33, 62
Point de Quilmes, 9, 13, 72, 80
Popham, Sir Home Riggs, xii-xiii, 2-9, 17-19, 25-7, 39, 41-3, 46, 48, 66, 122, 125-6, 128
Pueyrredon, Juan Martin de, 21-2, 24, 26, 31-2, 38-9
Quintana, Hilarion de la, 16-17, 28, 33-4, 90
Ratones, island of, 54, 58

Raymond, Lieut. Baptiste, 33
Recova, the, 12, 30, 32, 91
Reduction, 13-15, 75-6, 79-81, 143-4
Regiments: British
Cavalry: 6th Dragoon Guards, 73, 109-111. 9th Light Dragoons, 47, 67, 71, 91, 109-111. 17th Light Dragoons, 69, 77, 78. 20th Light Dragoons, 4, 17, 73. 21st Light Dragoons, 5, 73
Infantry: 5th Regiment, 77, 86, 91, 94-5, 97, 111. 6th Regiment, 4. 13th Regiment, 64. 14th Regiment, 64. 24th Regiment, 5. 36th Regiment, 64, 73, 78, 80, 86, 91, 100-101, 111, 143-5. 38th Regiment, 5, 43, 49, 56-9, 67, 73, 75, 91, 96-7, 99, 111, 143-5. 40th Regiment, 52, 79, 113. 45th Regiment, 42, 91, 104, 106-7, 111, 116. 47th Regiment, 19, 73. 52nd Regiment, 42. 54th Regiment, 5. 60th Regiment, 64. 65th Regiment, 45. 69th Regiment, 4. 71st Regiment, 4-6, 14-17, 21, 29-30, 32, 38, 61, 108, 110, 117-118, 143-5. 72nd Regiment, 5. 73rd Regiment, xi. 75th Regiment, 45. 87th Regiment, 52, 56-7, 75, 91, 94-5, 97, 99, 110-111, 116, 143-5. 88th Regiment, 5 73, 80, 91, 101-3, 108, 110-11, 117, 144-5. 89th Regiment, 65, 73. 93rd Regiment, 5. 95th Rifles, 91-2. 103rd Regiment, 42. Royal British South American Militia, 73. St. Helena Infantry, 6, 14, 21, 30, 61. Royal Engineers, 31, 147
Regiments: Spanish
Batallon de Marina, 39. Batallon de Naturales, 39. Pardos y

Morenos de Infanteria, 39.
Blandengoes de Buenos Aires,
26. Compania de Granaderos
de Infanteria, 39. Cuerpo
Arribenos, 39, 88. Cuerpo
de Artilleria de Indios, 39.
Pardos y Morenos, 39. Cuerpo
de Esclaves, 39. Cuerpo
de Husares Voluntarios,
51-2. Cuerpo de Patricios,
39. Cuerpo de Patriotas de
la Union, 39. Cuerpo de
Quinteros o Labradores, 39.
Dragones de Buenos Aires,
26, 128, 139. Dragones del
General, 129. Escuadron
auxiliar de Caballeria de la
Maestranza de Artilleria, 39.
Escuadron de Carabineros
de Carlos IV, 39. Escuadron
de Migueletes de Caballeria,
39. Husares de Pueyrredon,
39. Husares Cazadores o
Infernales, 39. Real Cuerpo
de Artilleria, 26. Regiment
Fijo de Buenos Aires, 128,
139. Regimiento Infanteria
de Buenos Aires, 26, 51.
Regimiento de Montevideo,
44. Voluntario Caballeria de
Montevideo, 44. Voluntarios
de Caballeria de la Colonia, 26.
Voluntarios de Infanteria de
Montevideo, 26.
Renny, Captain, 56
Residencia, 35, 91, 104, 106-7, 110-
111, 113-14, 116, 124
Retiro, 12-13, 29, 31, 88, 94, 115-16,
120, 145
Ridge, Captain, 98
Rio Chuelo, 15-17, 76, 79, 82-2, 84,
86-7, 113
Roache, Maj. Philip Gideon, 88-9
Rondeau, General Jose de, 128-9

Rosario, 55, 58
Saavedra, Cornelio, 88, 105
Saldannah Bay, xii
Salta, 62
San Antonio de Areco, 39
San Benito, 11
San Carlo, fight at, 44, 88
San Ignacio, 62
San Juan, 38, 55
San Luis, 38
San Martin, Jose de, 129
San Pedro, 69
Santa Fe, 51
Santa Rosa, 62
Saratea, Martin de, 25
Ships:
  Belliquesque, xii. Charwell,
  49. Diadem, xii, 9, 26, 47.
  Diomede, xii, 9. Elisa, 129.
  Encounter, xii, 49-50. Etrusco,
  3. Fly, 47, 72, 76, 147. Iasthma,
  29. La Voluntaire, 5. Leda, 12,
  54. Narcissus, xii, 8, 18, 41-2.
  Nercide, 47. Ocean, 6. 8. Orion,
  12. Reina Luisa, 12. Rodney, 3.
  Thisbe, 65, 67.
Smith, Harry, 57, 111, 125, 127
Sobremonte, Marquis de, 12-13,
16-17, 36, 40, 44, 51-2, 55, 58-9,
127, 139
Squire, Capt. John, 115, 147
St. Domingo, convent of, 108
St. Helena, 6-7, 19, 48, 71
Sterling, Admiral, 48, 52
Stopford, Commodore, 47
Suarez, Bernado, 51
Thompson, Captain, 27, 72, 76
Tippoo Sultan, xi, 42
Tolley, Major, 114
Trellis, Captain, 21
Trotter, Maj. 56, 108, 146
Tucuman, 38
Vandeleur, Maj. Richard, 101-103,
108, 111

Varela, Jacob, 88, 94, 97

Vassal, Colonel, 43, 56-78

Velazco, Bernado, 81-3, 86

Vittoria, battle of, 127

Waterloo, battle of, xiii, 127

Wellesley, Sir Arthur (Wellington,
    Duke of) xii-xiii, 3-4, 45-46,
    127, 129

White, William, 82, 85, 91

Whitelocke, Lieut-Gen. John, 46,
    61-74 passim, 75-80, 84-92, 99,
    102-4 107, 109-10, 114-121, 123-
    6, 128, 130, 134-7, 143

Whittingham, Capt. Sir Samuel,
    90, 110, 113-4, 122, 147

Windham, William, 45-7